12

Candles
of
Grace

Candles
of
Grace

Disciples Worship
in Perspective

by
Colbert S. Cartwright

Chalice Press
St. Louis, Missouri

All scripture quotations, unless otherwise indicated, are from
the *New Revised Standard Version Bible*, copyright 1989, Division of Christian Education of the National Council of the
Churches of Christ in the USA. Used by permission.

Quotations marked RSV are taken from the *Revised Standard
Version of the Bible*, copyright 1946, 1952, © 1971, 1973, Division
of Christian Education of the National Council of the Churches
of Christ in the USA. Used by permission.

Library of Congress Cataloging-in-Publication Data

Cartwright, Colbert S., 1924-
  Candles of grace : disciples worship in perspective / by
  Colbert S. Cartwright.
1. Christian Church (Disciples of Christ)—Liturgy.   2. Public
worship.   I. Title.
BX7325.C27 1992   264' . 0663   91-29002
ISBN 0-8272-0461-2

Printed in the United States of America

Contents

Preface

The Disciples of Christ began in large part as an early nineteenth-century American frontier effort to renew the church's worship. There were other concerns, of course, such as a drive toward the unity of the church and a vigorous affirmation of human liberty. But when they talked about the restoration of the New Testament church, the church's worship was often foremost in their minds.

This is apparent from countless letters printed in the publications edited by leaders of the movement. With great excitement people wrote in to tell of the formation of new congregations. Typical of what they reported is a letter that appeared in *The Millennial Harbinger* from Alexander Reynolds of Glasgow, Kentucky, dated March 26, 1833. Describing a new church he excitedly reported: "They have adopted the New Testament for their only guide in all matters of faith and manners—meet every Lord's day for the purpose of refreshing their memories with the incidents of Calvary—for edifying one another, and keeping up all the forms of worship instituted by Jesus and the Apostles."[1]

Today we would call this a movement for liturgical renewal. The most fundamental aspects of worship were reexamined in the light of how the church worshiped in New Testament times. Searching for the essence of that early experience and practice, congregations believed they could renew the sources of worship in their day. In the process they became pioneers in liturgical reform—lifting up aspects of liturgical faith and practice that today are at the heart of ecumenical discussion.

The Christian Church (Disciples of Christ) traces its roots back to several Presbyterian ministers who were disturbed by what they found on the American frontier in the early 1800s. They saw the tremendous challenge of the church to meet the spiritual needs of these sturdy pioneers as they moved westward to tame the wilderness and establish homes.

The various church bodies seemed ill equipped to do what was needed. Preoccupied with doctrinal disputes as to who had the true church, they fought among themselves rather than centering upon the spiritual needs of the people.

The frontier at this time was western Pennsylvania, western Virginia, Ohio, and Kentucky. The United States had recently adopted a remarkable Constitution, and with great optimism settlers moved westward to start new lives with fresh hope.

Within this context, these Presbyterian ministers began a movement to unite Christ's fragmented church. The basis for unity would be a fresh grasp of how Christ and his apostles ordered the church in New Testament times. That which was commonly taught and practiced then would become normative for their church life. Uniting in essential matters, congregations (and members) would be free to express a variety of opinions and practices according to their own wisdom.

Today, of course, we know this was a naive understanding of the church. A careful study of the New Testament reveals a multiplicity of practices and traditions. Church history relates many different understandings of various reformers as to what a return to pristine Christianity would mean. So Christ's church is still divided and the ecumenical search for church union continues.

But the rich heritage remains with us of a frontier people who sought afresh to renew the church through reappropriating the apostolic faith and practice. They were getting back to basics. This was true in regard to worship.

As Disciples seek today to make worship more vital, we would do well to revisit our heritage. The need is to look back and reclaim that history. Worship inevitably remains unfocused when we forget the paths our journeys have taken. Identity is grounded in memory.

The purpose of examining the old ways is not to copy them but to enter into dialogue with them. It is through such conversing with our forebears that we gain fresh insights and are challenged to find new ways of expression today. To some degree we are what we are today because of who we were in times past. We need to understand how we got that way in order to give responsible shape to our own future.

Being a Disciples pastor concerned for the vitality of worship, I have served on Disciples and ecumenical worship commissions, done graduate studies in worship, and led workshops in this field. When I was asked by the Association of Disciples Musicians to give major presentations of Disciples worship at their annual workshop, I agreed, as an opportunity for me to steep myself once again in our early Disciples heritage.

This required me to delve back into the brittle and dusty pages of the journals edited by our Disciples forebears. Someone has observed that Disciples did not have bishops. Rather they had editors. It was not bishops that guarded the faith and practice of these congregations. Rather, congregations were guided in faith and practice by reading the respected studies and observations of such ministerial editors as Thomas Campbell and his son, Alexander, writing from the western parts of Pennsylvania and Virginia. Congregational leaders sought guidance from journals edited by Barton W. Stone in Kentucky and Walter Scott in Ohio. They sometimes wrote letters of inquiry to these editors seeking counsel as to church practice. The printed answers of the editors often became the norms of church practice.

For me this was not simply an antiquarian search of old things. Rather, it was an opportunity to hear what our forebears had to say as it might apply to those who lead worship today. I found it a fascinating adventure and invite you to share in that dialogue within the setting of your own worship.

I was particularly struck by our forebears' insistence that worship belongs to the people. Looking back to New

Testament times, they saw worship centered not in an
ordained clergy but in a worshiping community. Looking
to their own worship on the frontier, they claimed it as
their own. Though generally respectful of clergy and lay
elders, they resisted any effort by them to control how they
worshiped. As a people of God centering life in Christ, they
believed they were competent to read the New Testament
for themselves and shape their worship accordingly. The
congregation staked its claim to Lord's Day worship. It
was to be their worship—the worship of the people.

In quoting our forebears, I have found myself uncom-
fortable with their sexist language, but I have decided to
leave their words as they gave them to us. The reader who
finds this a problem may want to turn first to my own
understanding of this matter in chapter 6. Because these
quotations are not easily found in Disciples literature, I
have noted their sources. I trust this will not distract from
the reading.

Portions of this book's material were presented at the
1988 workshop of the Association of Disciples Musicians in
Oklahoma City. Some of these thoughts have appeared in
articles I have written for *Mid-Stream* and *Impact*. I have
also presented the results of some of my research in a
videotape titled "A Dialogue on Worship with the Disciples
Founders," produced by the Division of Homeland Minis-
tries of the Disciples. To all who have encouraged me in
this endeavor, I am profoundly grateful. Kay Bessler-
Northcutt has been a source of strength, affirming me and
the possibilities of this book when I saw no way of complet-
ing the project. I particularly express appreciation to two
colleagues in ministry with whom I have delighted in
working—Quita Scarborough and Nancy DeWees. Apart
from their initial confident reassurance, this book would
not have been written.

Note

1. *The Millennial Harbinger*, Vol. 4, 1833, p. 236.

1

Becoming a People for Worship

Late in life Barton W. Stone reminisced what it was like to worship on the American frontier in the early decades of the nineteenth century. He recalled it was common in those times for "men, women, and children, to walk six or seven miles to a night meeting." Even "the darkest nights did not prevent them," he said, for "they tied up bundles of hickory bark, and left them by the way at convenient distances apart. On their return they lighted these bundles, which afforded them a pleasant walk." He added, "Many have I baptized at night by the light of these torches."[1]

Probably Stone's good old days, as ours, were never quite so good as he remembered them. I suspect mothers and fathers with lead-weight dozing children to carry, were not particularly enthralled by this Currier and Ives painting that Stone painted.

Yet we do marvel at the sheer determination our Disciples forebears exhibited in not only toiling to clear their lands to make a home and living, but to build a meeting house, establish a congregation, and gather each Lord's Day for worship. Something deeply impelled them to draw together with other Christians into something they called a church and to do what churches do: worship.

We wonder what it was that drew these rugged women and men together on a Sunday in the face of the frontier's hard realities. Why was worship so vitally important that after hard physical labor each week they expended every effort to gather for public worship? A search for that answer may help us today to grasp afresh what worship means for us. Though our skies are lit by sodium vapor and neon, we, too, live in bewildering times. It's still "a jungle out there." And we, too, must decide what is worth the devotion of our lives.

There is no going back to duplicate our forebears' worship. Yet, our church today is a natural outgrowth of how those before us understood the church and its life together. Human nature remains rather constant, and the gospel of yesterday is the same good news we have today.

We can learn from those who have gone before us. We can understand why we tend to do things in a "Disciplish" way, why we resonate to some ways of worship more than to others. In understanding how we "got that way," we shall know better what to do now.

The Assembly of the Summoned

Basic to worship is a community. Imagine what it would be like to be a member of a church that had everything but services of worship. It might have fellowship groups, and service projects and committee meetings and bake sales and, yes, those inevitable board meetings. But worship would be regarded as only something to be done alone—between you and God and a sunset. Would you want to join such a church?

Men and women on the frontier knew what it was to face God alone in the isolation of wilderness existence. God was real to them in their daily living. But they yearned to gather together with one another to worship God.

In words we today would want to make more inclusive, Campbell wrote: "Man is a social animal. As the thirsty hind pants for the brooks of water, so man pants for society congenial to his mind. He feels a relish for the social hearth and the social table; because the feast of sentimental and congenial minds is the feast of reason. Man, alone and solitary, is but half blessed in any circumstances. Alone and solitary, he is like the owl in the desert, a pelican in the wilderness. The social feast is the native offspring of social minds."[2]

Our mothers and fathers in the faith traveled long distances to church that they might no longer remain only half-blessed. To be fully blessed is to give and receive blessings from one another.

Pioneering individualists that they were, they saw the church as a voluntary association of Christians who with common mind and purpose covenanted to share life together. But though it seemed like just an ordinary group of volunteers, they knew the church was different. They heard a call from beyond themselves to come together and to center upon the one who called.

The church has always understood itself in this way. The basic meaning of the word *church* in Hebrew is the assembly of those who are summoned. Basically a secular term, which could refer to those who were called up for military service, it took on special meaning when the one who summoned was declared to be God. The church is God's assembly. The church may gather as volunteers of like-minded folk, but they stand in the presence of one who has called them together. Within God's assembly, each member loses something of his or her own rugged individualism. The members become a people of God. They attend to the one who has called them.

Jesus Christ is the gift of God by which believers come fully to know God. The church belongs to Christ. It is Christ who summons God's people to gather in worship. By centering upon Christ, we focus upon God. Somehow the Jesus we know in scriptures and through faith is so transparent to God that in knowing him we know God. Jesus the Christ is both our best image of God and our finest picture of what it means to be human. This happens through the power of the Holy Spirit. The Holy Spirit is the means by which God communicates and extends the presence of Christ into the present moment.

The church is the assembly of Christ that believes in him. When Jesus asked his disciples, "Who do you say that I am?" Peter responded, "You are the Christ, the Son of the living God" (Matthew 16:15–16, RSV). Jesus said, "On this rock I will build my church" (Matthew 16:18, RSV). Christ is the bedrock of faith.

The evangelist Walter Scott dubbed Peter's confession "the Golden Oracle."[3] It was so central to his own faith that Scott "wrote with chalk, in large letters, over the door of his academy, in the inside, the words 'Jesus is the Christ.'"[4] Basic to all ordinances is the confession of faith that Jesus is the Christ, the son of the living God. Such a confession is more than a creedal assent. It is a life commitment.

Alexander Campbell said that faith is a "trusting in Christ," a "hearty reliance upon him for salvation."[5] His colleague in ministry, Robert Richardson, wrote that faith is "a receiving Christ himself—a trusting in Christ, in all the grandeur of his personal character."[6] It is by centering faith in God's son, Jesus the Christ, that one worships God.

The Centrality of the Lord's Supper

Alexander Campbell from his study of scriptures concluded that worship in the early church centered around the Lord's Supper. He observed that "the primary intention of the meeting of the disciples on the first day of the week was to break bread."[7] He called attention to these words from Acts 20:7: "On the first day of the week, when we were gathered together to break bread..."(RSV). Further, the Acts of the Apostles relates that following Pentecost Christ's followers "devoted themselves to the apostles' teaching and fellowship, to the breaking of bread and the prayers" (Acts 2:42, RSV). References to "the breaking of the bread" were interpreted to be a shorthand expression for observing the Lord's Supper.

The great significance of this declaration lay not in how frequently the Lord's Supper should be observed—once a month, quarterly, or weekly. Rather, Campbell was getting to the core of the nature of Sunday public worship. He was reaching back to the intention of gathering in the first place. He was refocusing the very nature of what it means to worship God.

As early as 1812 Alexander Campbell's father, Thomas, declared that "New Testament worship ceases when the Lord's Supper is not observed every Lord's day."[8] That was an extreme position, which inappropriately put in question the validity of those who worshiped differently. But such a statement expresses the depths of conviction as to the very nature of worship. The intention of Sunday public worship is to gather about the table at which the risen Christ presides.

Alexander Campbell, explaining the centrality of the Lord's Supper in worship, commented: "It was the design of the Savior that his disciples should not be deprived of this joyful festival when they meet in one place to worship God. It will appear (if it does not already) to the candid reader of these numbers, that the New Testament teaches that every time they met in honor of the resurrection of the Prince of Life, or, when they assembled in one place, it was a principal part of their entertainment, in his liberal house, to eat and drink with him. He keeps no dry lodgings for the saints—no empty house for his friends. He never made his house assemble but to eat and drink with him."[9]

Campbell explained: "As bread and wine to the body, so it strengthens his faith and cheers his heart with the love of God. It is a religious feast; a feast of joy and gladness."[10] This is Campbell's basic description of what happens when

Christians assemble to worship. Is worship so understood, he asked rhetorically, "a privilege, or a pain"?

When worship is conducted in the light of this understanding, something transcendent happens. Campbell pointed to this transcendent quality of worship in these words: "The church must view herself, if sincere in her professions, as 'an habitation of God through the Spirit,' as 'the pillar and support of the truth,' as 'the temple of God,' and as 'the gate of heaven.' Every one that speaks or acts must feel himself specially in the presence of the Lord, not as on other days or in other places. Not a thought must be entertained, not a word spoken, not an action performed, that would make the disciple blush, if the Lord Jesus was personally present. The Lord, indeed, 'is in the midst of them' if they have met in his name and according to his word."[11]

Lord's Day worship centers upon the conviction that through our worship we are uniquely confronted by the living presence of God. It is the realization of God's presence that gives meaning to all we do. And apart from this conviction, all talk about worship is pointless. Within the church Jesus Christ becomes the means of our knowing and testing the reality of our experience of God. It is here that God speaks to us and nourishes with abounding love.

With this understanding of the nature of worship we come to see the way in which worship belongs to the people. Campbell was absolutely clear that worship did not belong to the clergy but to the people who worship.

This belief stemmed from his understanding of the worshiping community as living out its existence within Christ's table fellowship. With Christ being truly present in their midst, it is Christ who presides at his table. The people gathered at Christ's table find themselves all equal and all mutually empowered by the one who gives them food and drink. Within this eucharistic fellowship they are made Christ's people. Alexander Campbell declared: "The community, the church, the multitude of the faithful, are the fountain of official power....But the body of Christ, under him as its head, animated and led by his Spirit, is the fountain and spring of all official power and privilege."[12] We refer to this as believing in the priesthood of all believers.

Campbell strongly stated that every Christian should feel the heavy weight of shared responsibility for her or his communal life. Emphatically he declared: "A Christian is by profession a preacher of truth and righteousness, both by precept and example. He may of right preach, baptize, and dispense the supper, as well as pray for all men, when circumstances demand."[13] He went on quickly to add that due to the practicalities of life some persons, rather than others, are designated to perform certain functions. Everybody's business tends to become nobody's business. Campbell's point is simply that worship belongs to the people. The people must assume their privileges and responsibilities.

Developing a Sense of Solidarity

Looking at worship this way we find that through the centering of life in communion with Christ those who voluntarily assemble together in his name take on a new identity. They are more than a collection of individual Christians. They have become Christ's people.

Gathering on a Lord's Day to meet their Lord, they begin to be reshaped both as a people and individually. There is a dynamic process that takes place between worshipers and the one who calls them.

Through worship the community develops a common mind that has power to transform. It is not the mind of the everyday world with its tortured and twisted values, but a transcendent mind—the mind of Christ. This was what the apostle Paul saw happening within his beloved assembly of Christ's folk at Philippi. He joyfully counseled them:

> Let the same mind be in you that was in Christ
> Jesus,
> who, though he was in the form of God,
> did not regard equality with God
> as something to be exploited,

but emptied himself,
    taking the form of a slave,
    being born in human likeness.

Philippians 2:5–7

Coming about the Lord's Table and meeting the living Christ, this people take on a new lifestyle of serving others as well as being served. With humility they look to the interests of others and affirm one another's well-being.

In a like manner this community that communes with Christ becomes a power for reconciliation. The apostle Paul says something dramatically happens when Christ is at the center of this assembly. He reminds the fellowship of Christ at Corinth: "So if anyone is in Christ, there is a new creation: everything old has passed away; see, everything has become new! All this is from God, who reconciled us to himself through Christ, and has given us the ministry of reconciliation" (2 Corinthians 5:17–18). Each Sunday Christ is reconciling his people afresh to himself and reconciling them anew to one another.

Seeing worship in this light we find that the church is not just a voluntary group composed of like-minded people. This community is a called-together body whose members are bonded together through their common fellowship with Christ. It is composed of individuals with a wide variety of minds and temperaments and values. Their commonality lies not in their likeness but in their all seeking the mind of Christ. Out of their diversity they find ways of mutual service to others. And, of course, the church is not made up of perfect people, but, rather, of human beings with flaws and rough edges and generous portions of willfulness. What on earth can hold such persons together within a single community? Only the down-to-earth God working in Jesus the Christ who has brought reconciliation with the divine and who effects reconciliation ever and again—week after week—among God's people.

As the apostle Paul's experience reveals, these Christ communities are all still in the process of being formed.

They have the mind of Christ and are seeking to attain to it. They are a servant people and are still learning what it means to serve. They are reconciled to God and to one another, but at the same time working to make that reconciliation a reality in their daily existence. Every Sunday brings with it new concrete instances of uncompleted tasks to be done. The one who calls us together calls us ever afresh to a discipline to become his holy community of love.

This is God's community chosen to be a blessing to the nations. The assembly is sent out in mission to the world. Having experienced something of the power of God's reconciling love within its fellowship, it seeks to be a reconciling people in the affairs of everyday life. Knowing something of God's benediction of peace, it seeks to establish a shalom of love and justice among all God's creatures. Having prayed, "Thine is the kingdom, the power and the glory" in church, worshipers dare to confront all systems and powers in the world that usurp God's ultimate authority.

The prophets had a disconcerting way of judging the worship of God's people. Observing those who assembled to worship, Amos recognized their callousness toward the poor, the neglected, and the exploited. These very worshipers were conspirators in the crimes of existence. There was no congruence between word and deed, between pious pronouncement and righteous action. With holy indignation Amos cast the whole of worship in question. Speaking in God's name he said:

> I hate, I despise your festivals,
> and I take no delight in your solemn
> assemblies.
> Even though you offer me your burnt offerings
> and grain offerings,
> I will not accept them;
> and the offerings of well-being of your fatted
> animals
> I will not look upon.

Take away from me the noise of your songs;
   I will not listen to the melody of your harps.
But let justice roll down like waters,
   and righteousness like an everflowing
      stream.

Amos 5:21–24

I once heard a minister who had devoted his life to working among the poorest of the poor in Chicago say that worship is like a magnificent algebraic formula. It is filled with a multitude of plus marks and times signs. But the whole of it is enclosed by a bracket with a minus sign in front of it. That minus sign in front negates all the good the brackets contain. In the context of his worship that minus sign was racial injustice. Until the church removed that minus sign, all its glorious worship was for nought. There are surely minus signs other than race that negate the worship of God's assembled people.

The point is that worship cannot be detached from who the worshipers are both within the assembly and as they take their places in the world's daily life. Issues of apartheid, race, sexism, public education, prison reform, ecology, war, drugs, and corruption in business, as well as politics, all are indissolubly connected to our worship.

That connection has to do with solidarity with all God's creation. Those who worship the Christ who was given that the world may have life sense not only their own solidarity with those gathered around the Lord's Table locally, but also with sisters and brothers around the world who are determined to bless all existence.

The binding power of this worshiping community gathered about the Lord's Table is beautifully expressed in the earliest description we have of the Lord's Supper. In the Didache, dating back at least to the second century, the instructions are: "On the Lord's day, come together, break bread, and give thanks, having first confessed your transgressions, that your sacrifice may be pure. But let none who has a quarrel with his companion join with you until they have been reconciled, that your sacrifice may not be defiled." Assembled at the time of the breaking of the bread the one presiding says: "As this broken bread was scattered upon the hills, and was gathered together and made one, so let thy Church be gathered together into thy kingdom from the ends of the earth; for thine is the glory and the power through Christ Jesus for ever." At the Lord's Table we envision the full bringing together of all God's people.

Congregational worship is incomplete without this sense of future yet to be fulfilled. The apostle Paul concluded his passing on the Lord's Supper tradition by saying, "For as often as you eat this bread and drink the cup, you proclaim the Lord's death until he comes" (1 Corinthians 11:26). We experience the reconciling power of God's love only in part. This keeps us humble before God and before one another. Together we look forward to the full completion of God's creation.

A Church Home Within God's Family

In thinking about worship, first there is a community. It is the community of Christ that gathers for worship. It is the community that owns and expresses its worship.

Attending Sunday worship is not a drop-in matter of picking up a few needed personal items from the convenience store. It is not coming into the church with a consumer mentality looking for bargains. Though worship does meet our personal needs, perhaps our greatest personal need is to belong to a transcendent community that centers life in God. We yearn for a vital community in which God is known and loved and served. We want to share in such a fellowship—receiving, yes, but giving as well. It is through worship that we find a church home within the family of God.

When our Disciples forebears thought about worship, they at times became lyrical. So, we find Walter Scott penning in his diary: "Lord's Day, Dec. 3, 1848. The great festival—God's great festival; the best of all the seven. What a delight is the Lord's day! Crowded with the grand deeds of Christ—his death, resurrection, and ascension to heaven—it awakens in the soul all the resplendent recollections of the kingdom of God."[14]

For our early forebears, worship was a festive occasion they did not want to miss. Within their frontier cabins they knew they were no lonely owls or pelicans, but sociable beings who yearned to come together to celebrate the reality of God in Christ Jesus. It's hard to have a festival all by yourself.

Notes

[1]John Rogers, *The Biography of Elder Barton Warren Stone, Written by Himself, with Added Reflections* (Cincinnati: J. A. & U. P. James, 1847), p. 74.

[2]Alexander Campbell, editor, *The Christian Baptist*. Revised by D. S. Burnett, from the Second Edition with Mr. Campbell's Last Corrections. Fifteenth edition (St. Louis: Christian Publishing Co., n.d.), p. 175.

[3]William Baxter, *Life of Elder Walter Scott* (Cincinnati: Bosworth, Chase & Hall, Publishers, 1874), p. 61.

[4]*Ibid.*, p. 64.

[5]Robert Richardson, *Memoirs of Alexander Campbell*. (Philadelphia: J. B. Lippincott & Co., 1868), I, p. 411.

[6]*Ibid.*, I, p. 272f.

[7]*The Christian Baptist*, p. 55.

[8]Quoted by John Lyle Miller, *The Sesquicentennial History: First Christian Church, Shelbyville, Kentucky (1830-1980)* (Frankfort, Kentucky: Tingle's Typesetting, 1981), p. 21.

[9]*The Christian Baptist*, p. 175.

[10]*Ibid.*, p. 175.

[11]"Order of the Church as Respects Worship," *The Millennial Harbinger*, Extra, VI, 8, (1835), p. 507.

[12]*The Christian System*, Second Edition, (St. Louis: Christian Board of Publication, m.d., 1839), p. 89.

[13]*Ibid.*, p. 87.

[14]Baxter, *Life of Elder Walter Scott*, p. 406.

2

Selecting the Ingredients for Worship

What does it take to have worship? We have seen that first it takes a community of believers who center their lives in God as known in Jesus Christ. We are not lonely owls or pelicans, but persons who are made for one another. We express our essential nature as social beings by gathering for worship.

Once you are gathered, what do you need for worship to happen? Sometimes when I look at how our Disciples forebears worshiped I am reminded of some lines from the Rubaiyat of Omar Khayyam which, taken out of context, summarize our needs: "A Jug of Wine, a Loaf of Bread—and Thou." We need bread and cup and the real presence of the Divine Thou—Christ in our midst. Disciples worship

13

centers in a table fellowship with the risen and present Lord.

One of my favorite vignettes of early Disciples worship comes in the form of a letter that appeared in *The Millennial Harbinger*. It poignantly shows something of what these early reformers of worship thought were the essentials for worship. G. W. Elley of Nicholasville, Kentucky, in 1833 wrote to tell of his congregation's being so unpopular in the community that it was barred from using the free town meeting house on a Sunday to hold its worship. He relates: "I was about addressing the people, standing upon the door sill, I was ordered not to do so in the lot, but knowing my privileges, I proceeded with my discourse. They used great violence....There was a large concourse of people....They took an humble seat upon the grass, and there we spread a cloth, and broke the loaf upon the green, and I do not know that I ever saw more solemnity. Their violence is aiding us much...."[1]

From this scene we find that having worship on the Lord's Day was important—something we might take for granted. A building, though preferred, was not essential, but a place to meet was—even if it was on the ground. There was a discourse—preaching. They shared in the breaking of the loaf—the Lord's Supper. Their solemnity bespoke the felt presence of that transcendent one who comes when people gather in his name and according to his teachings. They also were a people being shaped contrary to the culture about them—worshiping despite violent opposition by a society looking scornfully upon them.

That service undoubtedly included other elements of worship that G. W. Elley took for granted, feeling no need to describe them in detail. There would have been singing and scripture reading and prayers, we can be sure. In fact, we can learn from Alexander Campbell what was generally included in such services and why.

Ordinances as Means of Grace

Alexander Campbell, through careful study of the apostolic writings of the New Testament, identified "certain ordinances delivered to the church by her exalted Redeemer, which she is constantly to observe in all her meetings to worship him."[2]

Within the New Testament he found what he termed *ordinances* for the conducting of Christian worship. Ordinances are, as Alexander Campbell expressed it, "the traditions of the Holy Apostles who were commanded to teach the disciples to observe all things which the king in his own person had commanded them."[3] These instructions and practices are Christ's ordinances—his way of ordering the church and its worship. But these, he asserts, are the primary ordinances of worship.

When Campbell spoke of an order of worship he was not referring to the proper sequence of the acts of worship, but about what Christ's orders were—his ordinances. He believed that although some sequences would be better than others, this was a matter of adapting to circumstances rather than to a decree.

Having those necessary ingredients, a congregation may express them creatively according to what seems best under its circumstances. Upon listing the essentials, Campbell added: "But at what hour of the day, and in what sort of a house, and how often on the Lord's day the church should assemble; and whether she should first pray, sing or read the Living Oracles; and at what period of her worship she should do this, or that, are matters left to the discretion of the brotherhood, and to that expediency which a thousand contingencies in human lot and circumstances must suggest, and for which no unchangeable ritual or formulary could possibly have been instituted."[4]

Much more important was understanding the purpose of all these worship ingredients. When Alexander Campbell spoke of them as ordinances he had something quite specific in mind. For a church to be governed by ordinances may sound rather austere and legalistic. Is worship a matter of adherence to a set of rules and regulations?

Alexander Campbell thought of ordinances as the means by which a believer receives God's grace. The church through the centuries had regarded sacraments as this means of grace. Roman Catholics identified seven sacraments, but the leaders of the Protestant Reformation cut the number to two—baptism and the Lord's Supper.

When Campbell studied the New Testament he found it difficult to decide how many ordinances there were that conveyed God's loving forgiveness, God's nurturing and caring—God's grace. The problem was that Campbell saw the grace of God shining through every ordinance required of the church.

Campbell declared that "all the wisdom, power, love, mercy, compassion, or *grace of God* is in the ordinances of the Kingdom of Heaven."[5] Regardless of their number, Campbell says ordinances "are the means of our individual enjoyment of the present salvation of God."[6] Then he comes to the heart of the matter with italicized emphasis: *"God never commanded a being to do any thing, but the power and motive were derived from something God had done for him."*[7] Ordinances, rather than being a burden, are delightful expressions of a thankful heart. "These," he says, "are the means of our individual enjoyment of the present salvation of God."[8]

The context of Disciples worship, then, is a gracious God. These reformers affirmed with the apostle Paul that we are saved by grace through faith. We cannot earn God's favor. God with gracious love gave Jesus Christ to the world that the world may believe and be saved. This all happened before any of us came onto the scene. As Alexander Campbell remarked, it is solely by God's grace that Jesus "and all that he did, suffered, and sustained for our redemption" took place. Then emphatically he added, "This is all favor, pure favor, sovereign favor."[9]

God's grace is the context of worship. The gospel of American achievement, of earning your way to favor, of trying harder, becoming number one—all of this permeates the very air we breathe. Throughout the media there runs a common theme: "I saved myself the old-fashioned way. I earned it."

The worshiper centered in grace—the favor of God—comes before God empty-handed, exposing one's threadbare soul to God, discovering God's amazing grace. You know that at the very heart of life is not an impossible demand, but divine love. Within the faith community at worship you now are nurtured within a different culture from that of the world where, as Alexander Campbell said, "it is all favor, pure favor, sovereign favor." When the ingredients, or ordinances, of worship are understood as being grace-filled, the nature of worship takes on meaning with remarkably fresh clarity. Worship has purpose and relevance.

Worship Is Reflexive

The best word I have found to characterize this kind of worship is *reflexive*. It is worship that is objectively directed toward God, but has profound subjective meaning for the worshiping community. It is reflexive in the sense that it is in giving that you receive; it is through opening oneself toward God that God comes afresh into your life.

Thomas Campbell, that thoughtful pioneer who penned in 1807 *The Declaration and Address,* and who possibly was the movement's best educated and disciplined theologian, crafted quite early a careful statement about worship.

Typically, Thomas Campbell began by stating what he saw to be objectively true. He said, "The author and ultimate object of our holy religion, is the God and Father of our Lord Jesus Christ, by his Spirit, speaking in Christ and his holy apostles." The appropriate human response, he next stated, is "a correspondent faith." "Thus," he said, in the third place, "we worship the Father, through the son, by the Spirit, relying upon his teachings in and by the word, to lead us into all the truth which he has testified for our edification and salvation."[10]

That is how Disciples forebears viewed worship. Worship is "reflexive" in the sense that as Christians glorify God, known in Jesus Christ through the power of the Holy Spirit, the glory of God's countenance shines back into the Christians' lives to imprint God's image upon their hearts.

Worship is reflexive: God mirrors back to us that love we send forth toward him.

For Thomas Campbell and his associates, public worship was centered objectively upon God. "The ultimate object of our holy religion," he declared, "is the God and Father of our Lord Jesus Christ." In nineteenth-century America, often awash with sentimentality, Thomas Campbell centered worship not upon the feelings of the worshiper but upon God. Faith is the response of the worshiper confronted by the amazing love of God the Father revealed by the Son, Jesus the Christ. Worship begins with God coming to humankind—made known by the power of the Holy Spirit in the person of Jesus the Christ. Worship for Campbell was not the seeking out of God in worship. Rather it was the life of responsive faith centered upon God.

But worship does have benefits for worshipers. God has ordered worship—has given it a distinctive content— by which worshipers find, as Thomas Campbell expressed it, "edification and salvation."

Three Monumental Institutions

For Alexander Campbell, worship was a gift of God to humanity that it might remember the mighty acts of God's salvation. We are all too prone in life to forget what God has out of pure grace done to effect our well-being. Because this is so, God has established what Campbell called three "monumental institutions." They are designed by their very nature to recall the worshiper again and again to the God who has in Christ brought life to its fulfilling possibilities.

Like monuments, they not only remind you of some mighty deed that has been done in the past, but also call you to ponder the meaning of what was done in terms of life today. Recalling what was done back then gives you a different understanding and outlook today. Those who have visited the Vietnam Veterans Memorial in Washington D. C. have not only remembered the horrors of that war, but somehow have become reconciled to those who fought in that hapless war. The monument has elicited tears and effected reconciliation.

Campbell saw this kind of thing happening through God's three monumental ordinances. What God has done, of course, is the gospel—God's redeeming love given in Christ for a wayward world. These monumental ordinances all recall the life, death, and resurrection of Jesus Christ.

Campbell saw the New Testament church as confining itself, "in its severe simplicity, to three institutions commemorative of the past." Continuing, he writes, "The Lord's day, the Lord's supper and baptism have indeed of themselves a fitness to indicate or picture forth the facts which they commemorate, or the new relations into which the believer enters." They unobtrusively "guide the thoughts of the believer to the gospel facts, and fix his faith upon the person and work of Christ."[11]

Monuments are symbols grounded in history. They convey facts as to what has taken place. But they also express the essential meaning of what took place. They bespeak a testimony as to why these deeds are to be remembered. Alexander Campbell wrote: "The whole Christian doctrine is exhibited in three symbols—baptism, the Lord's supper, and the Lord's day institution."[12] Campbell described the way in which these three holy institutions serve their divinely instituted purpose as monuments to the gospel of Jesus Christ.

Baptism

"Baptism into Christ," Campbell declared, "is indeed, monumental of his death, burial and resurrection. Hence they who are dead to sin, are buried with him in Baptism; rise with him, from the symbolic grave to walk in a new life."[13]

Baptism is a reminder—a living memorial, if you will—that Christ died for our sins and was raised to be made right before God. Campbell declared: "Baptism as administered by the primitive church, was a monumental evidence of the three great facts of man's redemption from sin, death, and the grave, by the death, burial and resurrection of Christ."[14] That is the doctrine proclaimed in the action of baptism.

But through this monument, this saving action takes place in our day and time through the power of the Holy Spirit. That once-and-for-all Christ event becomes living doctrine in the lives of those who believe and make that holy story their own through being baptized. Campbell described the monumental implications of baptism for the believer in these words: "On presenting himself, the candidate confessed judgment against himself by admitting his desert of death for sin, and promising to die unto it; while confessing that Jesus died for our sins, was buried, and rose again for our justification. His immersion in water, and emerging out of it, was a beautiful commemorative institution indicative of the burial and resurrection of the Messiah."[15] In this fashion one follows the path that Jesus took and makes it one's own through discipleship.

For Disciples baptism is, as Thomas Campbell expressed it, "the very first instituted act of the obedience of faith." It is the first act of discipleship. Through baptism the believer "is openly declared to be of the household of faith and of the family of God, being baptized into 'the name of the Father,' of whom the whole redeemed family in heaven and earth is named; and into the name of the Redeemer, the Son, and heir of all things, who makes his people free; and into the name of the Holy Spirit, the sanctifier, the comforter, and perfecter of the saints...."[16]

Baptism is hearing the monumental story of God's sacrificing and abounding love in Jesus Christ and re-enacting it in the waters of baptism. The life of discipleship trails out of those waters. It is embodying a life of dying and rising to God; dying and rising to others. It is a life of joyful response to what the monument of baptism bespeaks.

It is not a lonely journey, for, as Thomas Campbell noted, one "is openly declared to be of the household of faith and of the family of God."

The mood of baptism is joy and gratitude. God has done for us what we cannot do for ourselves. Out of gratitude for God's gracious love, we share that love as much as we can with all humankind.

The Lord's Day

Sunday itself is a monument to the redeeming figure, Jesus Christ. Campbell wrote: "The Lord's day celebrates his triumphant resurrection; the greatest event that ever was inscribed on the records of time."[17] Something of the monumental meaning of the Lord's Day was expressed by Walter Scott: "Jesus Christ has graciously set apart the first day of the week as the day on which his disciples may attend to those institutions and by thus attending upon them they are kept constantly under their saving influence....Thus by observing the first day of the week to the Lord, the great facts of his death, resurrection, and second coming are kept constantly before the minds of his people. What glorious recollections does the name of the first day of the week revive in the memories of all the saints! Jesus Christ arose from the dead. In fain did death, hell, and the grave combine their influence to hold him a captive in chains. He arose a triumphant victor over death....What a glorious theme is this for christians to dwell upon! Oh! it is calculated to inspire every heart with gratitude; fill every mind with wonder, and attune every voice to the praise of God."[18]

The Lord's Day is a day for remembering. When properly understood, Sunday is not so much a cessation from labor as it is a proclamation of the gospel. It calls attention to the mighty acts of God in Jesus Christ. One observes the Lord's Day as one observes a monument. One moves in and around and about it, pondering the past and searching one's own soul in the light of those past events. It is dwelling in a sanctified time that, if properly observed, sanctifies all one's daily living.

As our forebears understood it, observing the Lord's Day is more than commemorating an ancient event. It is the means by which believers participate in what happened long ago. Through the power of the Holy Spirit, observing the Lord's Day enables one to break the power of sin and death in one's life. Resurrection day power becomes a reality for believer and community.

Recall that for early Christians Sunday was a workday, as it was for pioneers eking out a living from the wilderness. For them to rest meant, as one scholar has expressed it, "not in devoting one day, but every day to God, and in abstaining, not from work, but from sin."[19] Its great significance lay in what the day commemorated—preeminently, the resurrection of Jesus Christ.

The first day of the week is called the Lord's Day in commemoration of the risen Lord. This one is Lord of all the days. It looks forward to the day of the Lord when all creation shall be fully restored by the reconciling love of God in Jesus Christ.

Sunday, then, is a cause for celebration. Sunday, far from being a day for somber thoughts, was regarded as a day of festival. Today we think of Christmas and Easter as festive occasions. This was not so for these pioneering Christians. God had through mighty acts of salvation sanctified Sunday so that every Sunday was a festal occasion. Nothing could top that seven-day cycle of remembrance—the Lord's Day. Sunday joyfully pictures forth that which is commemorated.

Since the Lord's Day is at its heart a festival, then it is apparent that its central purpose is for the assembling of God's people about their risen Lord. It is the Lord's Day, not ours. "There is the Lord's day, the Lord's table, the Lord's house, and the Lord's people," Alexander Campbell declared. It is all of one piece—one mighty monument.[20]

The Lord's Supper

Alexander Campbell called the Lord's Supper "the great ordinance of the day of the Resurrection." At the heart of congregational Sunday worship is the gathering of a community of Christ in fellowship to partake of the Lord's Supper. The Lord's Supper is monumental.

Just as baptism by its actions proclaims the good news of the life, death, and resurrection of Christ, so the Lord's

Supper in bread and cup recalls God's saving acts. Through the weekly observance of the Lord's Supper one recalls the story by which one entered the church. It is the same old story that must never be forgotten. So the church is given the Lord's Supper as a monument of remembrance.

The Lord's Supper recalls the saving story. It stands in itself as a proclamation of the church's faith in a living Savior. It is there even on those Sundays when a congregation seems to be going through an empty act. It is there, possibly a neglected monument for the moment, but available to remind those who wonder why they have gathered.

Just as in baptism, the Lord's Supper has the power not only to remind, but also to give us access to God in the living Christ. In the remembering, God becomes present to us and changes us. In the recalling of the story, God writes it afresh within the lives of God's people.

For Alexander Campbell, the Lord's Supper was a deeply personal and transforming experience. "Upon the loaf and upon the cup of the Lord," Campbell said, "in letters which speak not to the eye, but to the heart of every disciple, is inscribed, '*When this you see, remember me.*' Indeed, the Lord says to each disciple, when he receives the symbols into his hand, 'This is my body broken for *you*. This is my blood shed for *you*.'"[21]

Beneath these symbols the gospel message is freshly conveyed and received. Campbell stated: "The loaf is thus constituted a representation of his body—first whole, then wounded for our sins. The cup is thus instituted a representation of his blood—once his life, but now poured out to cleanse us from our sins. To every disciple he says, 'For *you* my body was wounded; for *you* my life was taken.' In receiving it the disciple says, 'Lord, I believe it. My life sprung from thy suffering; my joy from thy sorrows; and my hope of glory everlasting from thy humiliation and abasement even to death.'"[22]

The writing on the monument is now inscribed upon the monument of each believer's heart. More than words are written there. The picture of Jesus Christ is engraved within us. In these deeply personal moments, Campbell said the Lord's Supper "inscribes the image of God" upon the believer's heart. For him this was the moral impact of the gospel. Our lives are changed. The one who transforms us lives out his life within us to transform all of life.

Sharing in the Lord's Supper is not only personal but deeply social. Campbell emphasized that in serving "those lively emblems of the Saviour's love" to one another, the whole body of Christians is bound together in Christian love. Campbell was graphic and specific as to the communal power of sharing together in the Lord's Supper. He said: "Each disciple, in handing the symbols to his fellow-disciples, says in effect, 'You, my brother, once an alien, are now a citizen of heaven: once a stranger, are now brought home to the family of God. You have owned my Lord as your Lord, my people as your people. Under Jesus the Messiah we are one. Mutually embraced in the Everlasting arms, I embrace you in mine: thy sorrows shall be my sorrows, and thy joys my joys. Joint debtors to the favor of God and the love of Jesus, we shall jointly suffer with him, that we may jointly reign with him. Let us, then, renew our strength, remember our King, and hold fast our boasted hope unshaken to the end."[23]

Possibly Alexander Campbell's strongest expression of the social or corporate nature of the Lord's Supper relates to his insistence that there should be only one loaf on the table. He based this requirement upon the apostle Paul's words, "Because there is one loaf, we, the many, are one body; for we are all partakers of that one loaf" (1 Corinthians 10:17 *Living Oracles*). The loaf represents the physical body of Jesus Christ as well as the body of Christ—his church.[24] When the one loaf is dramatically broken during worship it serves as a monument to Christ's crucifixion. When the pieces are shared with all the church's members, they sense a fresh unity as all sharers in the one Christ. It is in this sense that the Lord's Supper is a monument to the intentional and essential nature of Christ's church.

Campbell so firmly believed in this ecumenical meaning of the breaking of the bread that he regarded it to be mandatory to have the one loaf and dramatically to break it within the congregation each Sunday. The whole spirit of the Lord's Supper is that of festivity. Campbell said that just as bread and wine are to the body, so they strengthen a Christian's faith and cheer the Christian's heart "with the love of God."[25] "It is a religious feast," Campbell declared, "a feast of joy and gladness."[26]

So, Campbell concluded, the Christian community has "its feasts and its joys, and its ecstasies too. The Lord's house is his banqueting place, and the Lord's Day is his weekly festival."[27]

It is when we understand the monumental nature of the Lord's Supper that we begin to catch the spirit of its observance. It is festive in celebration of the mighty saving acts of God. It's the kind of festival that makes you want to celebrate in words and song and dance. It is the celebration that comes at the end of victorious battle. But the monument reminds us that such victory has come through an awesome sacrifice—God's very self-giving in Jesus who was crucified at the hands of a cruel and rejecting world.

So Walter Scott, in his diary entry celebrating the glories of the Lord's Day, wrote of "the solemn gladness of the Lord's Supper." The spirit is that of rejoicing, but one stands in aweful wonder at what was done then and at what is here and now being done within the lives of those who assemble in Christ's name.

It is a challenge for Disciples to strike that contradictory balance in worship. Thoughtful Christians of other traditions marvel with gratitude that Disciples recovered for Protestants the centrality of the Lord's Supper for congregational Sunday worship. But we miss the festive note. Sharing in the Lord's Supper is to be taken with all seriousness. But when you take it seriously, you begin to hear the good news and you rejoice and you share that joy with your neighbor. The solemn remembrance turns into a glad meal of fellowship. You celebrate the unbounded love of God in Jesus Christ. And the joy becomes unbound as you worship.

Campbell pointed out that in these three monumental ordinances lie the rudimental elements of the whole means by which God has renewed life. "They are monumental," he said, "in the highest conception of the term, and comprehend all that is evangelically indicated in that sublime and beatific term, Redemption. This is, in all truth, a word of the most soul-stirring eloquence, indicative of all that can beautify, beatify and glorify man forever."[28]

Notes

[1]*The Millennial Harbinger*, Vol. IV (1833), 7, p. 329.
[2]*Ibid.*, Extra, VI, 8, (1835), p. 508.
[3]*The Christian Baptist* (1830), p. 656.
[4]*The Millennial Harbinger*, Extra, VI, 8, (1835), p. 509.
[5]*The Christian Baptist*, p. 186.
[6]*Ibid.*
[7]*Ibid.*, p. 187.
[8]*Ibid.*, pp. 187-188.
[9]Campbell, *The Christian System*, p. 188.
[10]"Essay on the Religion of Christianity," *The Christian Baptist*, p. 99.
[11]Richardson, *Memoirs of Alexander Campbell*, I, p. 407.
[12]*Ibid.*, I, p. 438.
[13]*The Millennial Harbinger*, Vol. 32 (1861), p. 250.
[14]Campbell-Rice Debate, 234, quoted by Jesse R. Kellems, *Alexander Campbell and the Disciples* (New York: Richard R., Smith, Inc., 1930), p. 262.
[15]*Ibid.*
[16]*The Christian Baptist*, p. 99.
[17]*The Millennial Harbinger*, Vol. 32 (1861), p. 250.
[18]*The Evangelist*, Vol. 4, #10, 1835, pp. 216-218.
[19]Quoted by J.J. von Allmen, *Worship: Its Theology and Practice* (New York: Oxford University Press, 1965), p. 219.
[20]*The Christian System*, p. 301.
[21]*Ibid.*, p. 331.
[22]*Ibid.*
[23]*Ibid.*
[24]*Ibid.*, p. 325.
[25]*The Christian Baptist*, p. 175.
[26]*Ibid.*
[27]*Ibid.*, p. 176.
[28]*The Millennial Harbinger*, Vol. 32 (1861), p. 250.

3

Giving Shape
to Worship

Although Alexander Campbell did not believe the New
Testament required a fixed ordering of the various elements of worship, he saw them all relating to the living
Christ who was truly present to those who worshiped.
Christ's presence was not dependent upon a divinely
required sequence of worship's elements, "though,"
Campbell quickly added, "in these there is an order which
is comely, apposite, or congruous with the genius of the
religion, and concerning which some things are said by the
apostles."[1]

Within these carefully stated parameters, Disciples
congregations have been free to set their own worship in
order. As to whether or not it has always been "comely,

apposite, or congruous with the genius of the religion" and in keeping with the admonitions of the apostles, there may be some question. Freedom sometimes becomes license; choices turn to whims.

In any case, Christ has undoubtedly been in their midst, regardless of the way Disciples ordered their worship. But, as Campbell indicated, some ways are better than others. A survey of patterns that have been common to Disciples in different periods of their history may be instructive.

Shaping According to Circumstances

During the very early years of this frontier movement, the order of worship varied considerably according to circumstances. In some cases a handful of Disciples gathered with no disciplined leadership and did the best they could. They generally were guided by Acts 2:42 and in some way "devoted themselves to the apostles' teaching and fellowship, to the breaking of bread and the prayers." They could do that whether or not they had an elder to lead them.

Many of these small worshiping congregations met weekly for the Lord's Supper, but had a preacher only once a month. When the elder came to preach, his sermon would come last, being added to what they usually did.

Under other circumstances, a congregation frequently met for edification on Lord's Day morning, shared in the Lord's Supper in the afternoon, and had preaching in the evening.

Quite commonly a congregation having a single Lord's Day service ordered its worship like this:

1. Invocation
2. One or two hymns
3. Reading of scriptures
4. Prayer
5. Hymn
6. Sermon
7. Invitation hymn

8. Lord's Supper
9. Hymn
10. Benediction

Sometimes the Lord's Supper was observed before the sermon, but that was the exception in the first fifty years of our history.[2] By 1920 an estimated two thirds of Disciples congregations ordered their worship to have the sermon to be the climax, rather than the Lord's Supper. The Disciples, always strongly influenced by the revival movement, joined other denominations in building worship up to the preaching of a fervid appeal to repent and believe. At the same time, churches began to be known for their "giants in the pulpit" with the sermon the main attraction. A third dynamic I remember from my own childhood in a parsonage: Devout members were scandalized by some members coming for the sermon and skipping out the door before communion. The Lord's Supper was tucked in before the sermon to end such deviant behavior.

Thus, quite commonly the order of worship by 1920 followed this pattern:

1. Opening praise
2. Scripture reading
3. Pastoral prayer
4. Lord's Supper
5. Offering
6. Sermon[3]

By the 1920s worship became heavily subjective with its main purpose being to instill religious feelings in those who came to worship. A prominent Disciples minister, concerned to enrich the congregation's Sunday worship, defined worship like this: "Worship is experiencing the sense of God."[4]

The literature and courses about Christian worship expressed this subjectivity in one of two ways: either as the *psychology* of worship or the *art* of worship. The prime question for ordering worship was how best to afford an individual the opportunity to "experience the sense of God." The practical problem with ordering worship psychologically or artistically is that subjectivity breeds multiple answers. One person's experience is as good as another's. It's all a matter of how you personally feel.

The experts in the psychology or the art of worship could not agree. One person believed worship should follow this sequence: (1) adoration, (2) communion, (3) dedication. But another person declared that worship should follow this pattern: (1) vision, (2) confession, (3) renewal, (4) dedication. G. Edwin Osborn in his widely used *Christian Worship: A Service Book* chose these four as the proper sequence: (1) an act of reverence, (2) an act of fellowship, (3) an act of dedication, (4) an act of renewal.

Who is right? It's all a matter of how you feel. But is there not some objective standard to be used? A strange thing happened. Isaiah's vision of God in the temple, related in Isaiah 6:1–8, became the widely accepted norm for contemporary worship both in Europe and in America. A Disciples minister by the name of W. S. Lockhart serves as an example of how Isaiah's vision was used. In the 1920s, Lockhart established a foundation to enrich Disciples worship. Referring to Isaiah's vision, Lockhart identified five stages of worship:

1. "I saw the Lord."   VISION
2. "Woe is me!"   HUMILITY
3. "Thy sins are forgiven." VITALITY
4. In the divine presence.   ILLUMINATION
5. "Here am I; send me."   DEDICATION[5]

Assuming for a moment that there is agreement on the psychological or aesthetic stages as found in Isaiah's vision, what items of worship fit under each heading? There has never been any consensus.

Many of our congregations still reflect some form of a psychological or aesthetic approach to public worship justified by Isaiah's vision.

In truth there is no reason why a worshiping congregation should construct its corporate worship in the light of

Isaiah's personal religious experience. It is never set forth in the Bible as a normative experience for public worship. When the attempt is made to do so, there is no compelling logic as to how contemporary worship should be ordered. Further, the whole motivation for its use was based on a false definition of worship. Worship is not "experiencing the sense of God."

Rather, worship is more objective in character. Thomas Campbell reminds us, "We worship the Father, through the Son, by the Spirit...." Worship is reflexive in the sense that in centering our attention upon God, God freely and abundantly attends to our needs. Christ's ordinances are the means by which we are brought to God and through which God touches us deeply, at the core of our being.

Learning from the Early Church

In reality what we intend to accomplish in congregational worship requires a strikingly different and stronger ordering of worship. For Disciples a normative Sunday worship service consists of a Christian community attending to the preaching of God's word and sharing in the Lord's Supper. That is basic. Neither of these was anticipated by the prophet Isaiah.

The question in developing Sunday worship is how best to order its various elements so that through a congregation's centering upon God as known in Jesus Christ, God's effectual grace can reflexively be received in the power of the Holy Spirit by those present.

According to the Campbells, God's grace uniquely comes through worship where the Lord's Supper characterizes all that is done. The partaking of the Lord's Supper dynamically affects all else that takes place.

How should such a "eucharistic fellowship"—a community centering its life in the Lord's Supper—shape and express its worship? We are discovering that although the New Testament does not give us a pattern, the church in its earliest centuries did develop a consistent pattern that has considerable merit today.

Studying these ancient accounts of early church worship, we find that normative worship always included the preaching of the word and the sharing in the Lord's Supper. Although there were local variations, the basic outline for ordering worship was consistent—consistent not by edict, but by the logic of what the early church understood to be the meaning of its worship.

Our earliest account of Christian worship comes to us from the middle of the second century. It was written by the apologist Justin to the Emperor Antoninus Pius. He wrote: "And on the day called Sunday there is a meeting in one place of those who live in cities or the country, and the memoirs of the apostles or the writings of the prophets are read as long as time permits. When the reader has finished, the president in a discourse urges and invites [us] to the imitation of these noble things. Then we all stand up together and offer prayers. And, as said before, when we have finished the prayer, bread is brought, and wine and water, and the president similarly sends up prayers and thanksgivings to the best of his ability, and the congregation assents, saying the Amen; the distribution, and reception of the consecrated [elements] by each one, takes place and they are sent to the absent by the deacons."[6]

In outline form, Justin's description fits this pattern:

THE SERVICE OF THE WORD
    Readings from the Gospels
    Sermon by the president
    Prayers by all the people, said standing

THE SERVICE OF THE LORD'S SUPPER
    Bread, wine, and water are brought in
    Extempore prayer of thanksgiving
    People's response: Amen
    Distribution and reception of elements

Amazingly, this basic order of Christian worship changed very little through the centuries. It was skewed by The Roman Catholic Church when it lost out the importance of preaching. It was skewed by Protestants who dropped out the normative celebration of the Lord's Supper each Sunday.

The Genius of Early Christian Worship

With the collapse of Isaiah's vision serving as a normative approach to ordering Christian worship has come a revival of interest in seeking out the genius of Christian worship. What was it like in the early church when Sunday worship normatively included the preaching of the Word and the partaking of the Lord's Supper?

The result of this study by Roman Catholics and Protestants alike has brought about one of the most far-reaching shifts in Christian worship in the history of the church. In the light of early Christian worship, The Roman Catholic Church in Vatican II pared back its worship to basics, expressed worship in the language of the people, returned the Bible to the people, and recovered preaching.

Concurrently with these changes in The Roman Catholic Church, Protestants in seeking to recover the genius of early Christian worship made their own revolutionary discoveries. Through their studies, the Protestants became convinced that the church is at heart a eucharistic fellowship. That is, the church is a community that is formed around the Lord at his table in thankful praise. The norm for congregational Sunday worship is to hear the word of our Lord from scripture and sermon and to share in the Lord's festival at his table.

These Protestants—Lutherans, Episcopalians, Methodist, Presbyterians, and such—realized that they had lost out from their normative worship the regular sharing in the Lords' Supper. In the rewriting of their orders of worship, all of these Protestant bodies are now following the basic pattern of the early church. Both the preaching of the word and the sharing in the Lord's Supper are normative for every Sunday. Protestant churches, unable to change worship by edict, are slower to reform. But they are including the Lord's Supper more frequently than they once did. They are working toward normative worship in which the word is preached and the Lord's Supper is shared each Lord's Day.

All of a sudden the world's light is shed upon the Disciples who have known that normative worship always includes the preaching of the word and sharing in the Lord's Supper. This has been Disciples practice since the first service held by the Campbells at Brush Run. So it is that liturgical scholar James F. White has commented that among Protestants, those in the Disciples tradition were the first people to recover the normative practice of including the sermon and communion in the Sunday worship service.[7] Among Protestants, the Disciples are regarded as having pioneered in liturgical renewal.

But Disciples, too, have been learning from this fresh turning to early Christian worship as setting the norm for worship today. We are learning that those in the early church were careful to structure their worship so it conveyed their intended meaning.

How you order your worship in sequence makes a statement in itself. When you order the various parts differently, you are also changing their meaning. We are learning that the very structure of worship itself is crucial in conveying meaning. Keith Watkins has been the foremost liturgical scholar among Disciples to make this point.[8]

To my mind, this manner of renewing Disciples worship is as fundamental to us as those remarkable renewing actions taken by the Roman Catholics and vast numbers of Protestants around the world. We cannot be smug about having known all along that word and cup belong together. We, too, need to recapture the remarkable dynamic that is involved when you take all of this seriously as the very means by which God shares God's grace with Christ's church.

Preaching and Then the Lord's Supper

One of the things we are learning from early Christian worship is first to preach the word and then to participate in the Lord's Supper. We were correct from the beginning in insisting that our reason for gathering in worship on the Lord's Day was to commune with our Lord about his table. What we often failed to understand was how preaching related to that.

A searching back to our roots in the early Christian centuries reminds us first that the gospel is proclaimed in word and then it is proclaimed in dramatic symbolism. The action of the Lord's Supper is symbolic only when the symbolism is clearly understood. First the gospel is preached and then it is enacted as we make it our own.

The Lord's Supper is not passive. It is something you decide to do. You may partake or not, as you choose. Worship is reflexive. It is centering wondrous attention upon our Lord and then receiving afresh that Lord back into our lives as we take the bread and eat, pick up the cup and drink. Our eating and drinking are in response to the gospel preached of Christ crucified and Christ raised from the dead.

It may sound irreverent, but there is a sense in which after hearing the gospel preached, we say at the Lord's Table, "I'll drink to that!" But that is not quite what happens. In reality, Christ confronts us in the gospel preached and then invites us to share fellowship with him through food and drink.

Looking at the sermon in this light, preaching every Sunday takes on eucharistic meaning. That is, it leads on to the climax of worship, which is sharing in the Lord's Supper. The sermon each week presents Christ to us in some specific aspect of his life and teaching, his sufferings, his death, his resurrection. The good news takes on specific shape of gift and demand. We see Christ differently according to the coloration of that day's gospel lesson. Then comes the invitation to share in Christ's life afresh.

When sermon and Lord's Supper are structured in this fashion, there is no need for someone to give a communion meditation to keep it from becoming stale ritual. The sermon as gospel proclaimed that day is the agenda for communion. Through scripture and sermon the worshipers have been confronted afresh by God's Word made flesh in Jesus Christ. Through the symbolic action of the Lord's Supper, the worshipers take action to receive God's Word as grace which comes to them that day through the living Christ who hosts that meal.

Wedding of Scripture and Sermon

The other dynamic that comes from early Christian worship to enliven our contemporary worship is the wedding of the reading of the scriptures with the sermon. Worship needs to be so ordered that it is quite clear to all that the minister is opening up the Holy Bible and seeking to let its light shine through the sermon.

During much of Disciples history, as in much of American Protestantism, the sermon was detached from the scripture. One reason was that topical preaching was in vogue. A minister picked a topic and then hunted up a text, or "pretext," from which to preach. When the vision of Isaiah became the outline, the scripture was not intended to relate to the sermon. Rather, it was to evoke a confrontation with the Holy God, high and lifted up. Scripture was selected to evoke the proper psychological religious feelings.

The fresh recovery of early Christian worship has brought with it renewed appreciation for God's revelation contained in the Bible and the value of preaching from it. Even before they became holy scriptures, the letters and gospels and acts of the apostles were circulated among the churches and read and expounded. They became the Bible because a worshiping people found them conveying to them the living Word of God.

Another sign of the astounding renewal of worship in our generation is the ecumenical recovery of the importance of the Bible in worship. For Roman Catholics it was hearing the scriptures read in English at worship. For Protestants it has been the recovery of systematic reading of the scriptures during a church year.

As a part of its liturgical reform, The Roman Catholic Church developed a lectionary on a three-year cycle. A lectionary is an ordered listing of scripture passages to be read in worship Sunday by Sunday throughout the church year. The Catholic lectionary provides for the reading of three scripture lessons each Sunday—a lesson from Hebrew scriptures, a lesson from an epistle (or Acts), and a Gospel lesson. It provides for the reading over a three-year period of most of the New Testament and significant portions of the Hebrew scriptures. There is a Psalm also designated for reading or chanting each Sunday.

The readings are designed for the Old Testament lesson to illumine in some fashion the reading of the Gospel lesson for the day. The epistles and Acts are read in series over a period of Sundays. Although these may serve as the basis for expository preaching, they may be regarded as simply scriptures with which the congregation needs to become familiar.

This Catholic lectionary was so well-done that American Protestant churches found that with some modifications it could serve them well. The result has been the production of what is called the *Common Lectionary*.[9] It is not uncommon to find across the land a wide variety of churches—Catholic and Protestant—all centering their worship on the common scripture readings for the day.

The adoption of scripture readings each Sunday in worship from the *Common Lectionary* has brought the Bible back to a central position in preaching. It is ironic that the Roman Catholics, from whom we claimed the Bible for the people in Protest, are the ones in our generation who have given the Bible in worship back to the Protestants. Particularly significant is the fact that a lectionary is based on a church year that celebrates the acts of God. Over a year's time, the church in its scripture readings rehearses God's actions in history.

Each year, one of the three synoptic Gospels is used as a basis for narrating the God-story lived out by Jesus the Christ. You begin with Advent, the promise of Christ's coming. You move on to Christmas with the birth of the Savior and on to Epiphany. You soon find yourself in Lent, recalling the sacrificial ministry of Christ, which led to his death on a cross. Then in jubilation you celebrate Christ's resurrection at Easter and his continuing ministry to his followers. Then Christ's Ascension arrives, followed by the pouring out of the Holy Spirit at Pentecost upon Christ's new community—the church.

All the while the worshiping congregation is hearing other portions of the Bible read. Particularly valuable is the manner in which the epistles are read straight through from beginning to end over a series of Sundays. The Gospel reading sets the tone for the day, but the preacher from time to time may depart from exposition of the Gospel to lead the congregation in a study over several weeks of an epistle. In any case, the people of God hear the word of God regularly as it comes from holy scriptures.

It is important to remember that the lectionary provides many ordinary Sundays in between these high Sundays of celebration of the life of Christ. These Sundays afford opportunities for the preacher to either follow the ordered lessons or to preach on other concerns. The lectionary is not a law to bind, but a discipline to assist. There is always the freedom to depart from it to deal with immediate pastoral or prophetic concerns.

Such an orderly reading of scripture is not foreign to the Disciples tradition. It was common for Walter Scott to preach straight through a single gospel over a period of many months.[10] Some local congregations were accustomed to having weekly readings from the Old Testament, the Gospel, and the epistles each Sunday—going straight through the Bible in that fashion, only omitting what was clearly unedifying, such as "the begats."[11]

So it is that many Disciples congregations have learned afresh to keep the scripture reading in close proximity to the sermon. They belong together. It is through both the scripture being read and the sermon being preached that Christ's community hears and proclaims God's word.

We begin now to see Disciples worship taking shape and order. The ancient church shows us the way. Justin put it well in the very beginning. First, "the memoirs of the apostles or the writings of the prophets are read as long as time permits. When the reader has finished, the president in a discourse urges and invites...." Then, second, "bread is brought, and wine and water, and the president similarly sends up prayers and thanksgivings to the best of his ability...." And Christ is made known to them afresh in the breaking of the bread.

This is an exciting time to be involved in the leadership of worship. We are a part of something new God is doing with us. God is breathing fresh life into the worship of Christ's church. It is happening in Catholic and Protestant churches alike.

God is reforming, reshaping, renewing our worship. God is breathing new life into that community that centers life in Christ about Christ's festal table. "Behold, I am doing a new thing," says our Lord. We are called to be ministers of God's renewal. Let us take a big breath—from God—and lead the way for this to happen right where we serve each Sunday.

Notes

[1]*The Christian Baptist*, p. 165.

[2]Edgar DeWitt Jones, "Architecture and Worship Among the Disciples," *The Shane Quarterly*, II, April-July 1941, p. 176.

[3]W. B. Blakemore, "Worship Among Disciples of Christ, 1920-1966," *Mid-Stream*, VII, 4 (Summer 1968), p. 53.

[4]G. Edwin Osborn, ed., *Christian Worship: A Service Book* (St. Louis: Christian Board of Publication, 1953), p. 6, footnote 1.

[5]W. S. Lockhart, *The Ministry of Worship* (St. Louis: Christian Board of Publication, 1927), p. 97.

[6]Justin Martyr, *First Apology*, chapter 67, found in Cyril Richardson, ed., *Early Christian Fathers* (Philadelphia: Westminster Press, 1953), p. 287f.

[7]James F. White, *Christian Worship in Transition* (Nashville: Abingdon, 1976), p. 68.

[8]See these books by Keith Watkins: *The Breaking of Bread* (St. Louis: Bethany Press, 1966); *The Feast of Joy* (St. Louis: Bethany Press, 1977); and Watkins, ed., *Thankful Praise* (St. Louis: CBP Press, 1987).

[9]See Peter C. Bower. ed., *Handbook for the Common Lectionary* (Philadelphia: Geneva Press, 1987).

[10]See Baxter, *Life of Elder Walter Scott*, p. 331.

[11]See John Allen Hudson, *Pioneers of Worship* (Kansas City: The Old Paths Book Club, 1947), p. 85ff.

4

Experiencing Lord's Day Worship

Disciples are, I believe, at a critical point in how we shape and express our Sunday public worship. Many Disciples congregations tinker here and there with their worship services without any real sense of what drives their inner purpose. They sense something is wrong. But they find it difficult to identify just what it is.

It is my observation that although our purpose in worshiping has changed in recent decades, worship services are not reflecting this change in outlook. Many services were shaped psychologically or artfully to induce a "feeling of the sense of God," as we saw in the previous chapter. The worship was ordered after a vision of the Old Testament prophet Isaiah, who "saw the Lord sitting on a throne, high and lofty; and the hem of his robe filled the temple" (Isaiah 6:1).

There is much to be learned from Isaiah's vision but, as I have attempted to make clear, the ordering of Christian worship is not one of them. That is a very personal and individualistic religious experience. The genius of Christian worship lies in another vision. It has to do with disciples gathered about their Lord at a table for communion with Christ and one another.

The Christian vision of worship is more nearly reflected in that simple story Luke tells of two dispirited disciples trudging back home to Emmaus from Jerusalem after the crucifixion. As they were walking along and lamenting what had taken place, a stranger joined them and asked them what was wrong. One of them, Cleopas by name, told the stranger about Jesus who held out such great hope for the coming of God's kingdom. But he had been arrested, convicted, and nailed to a cross to die. And now, three days later, there was talk of an empty tomb and his being alive. They told the stranger that they had gone to the tomb to see for themselves, but "they did not see him" (Luke 24:24). In response this stranger called them "foolish...and slow of heart to believe all that the prophets have declared!" So he "interpreted to them the things about himself in all the scriptures" (24:25,27).

As they came to Emmaus it was getting dark and the disciples begged him to stay with them. And then, Luke says, "When he was at the table with them, he took bread, blessed and broke it, and gave it to them. Then their eyes were opened, and they recognized him; and he vanished from their sight. They said to each other, 'Were not our hearts burning within us while he was talking to us on the road, while he was opening the scriptures to us?'" (24:30– 32). Then they ran back to Jerusalem to join the other disciples who greeted them with the words, "The Lord has risen indeed!" (24:34).

That, too, is a vision. Jesus Christ appears and disappears. But catch the pattern. Confused and dispirited disciples. (That could be us.) The scriptures are recited and expounded. (That could be us.) And Jesus then joins them in a meal. (That could be us.) When he took the bread, and blessed and broke it, and gave it to them, "their eyes were opened, and they recognized him" for a moment "and he vanished from their sight." (That could be us.) And they shouted, "The Lord has risen indeed!" (That could be us—on any Sunday where we worship.)

Shaping Worship According to Purpose

Catch something of the shape of Sunday public worship out of this new vision of the living Christ. First, the reciting of scriptures and interpreting them. After that, the breaking of the bread and intimate recognition of the Lord who has risen. Then rushing out the door to tell the good news.

What would our worship be like if this became a congregation's vision for worship? It would look very much like the Christians' worship Justin described in a letter to his emperor back in the middle of the second century. It is this shaping of worship to fit what Christians have been about from the beginning that is taking place in liturgical renewal. The contours of public worship among Roman Catholics and Protestants alike are being fitted more nearly to this Christian vision of interpreting the scriptures and supping with their risen Lord.

The question here is not one of authenticity of worship. Where two or three are gathered in Christ's name, there he is in their midst. Further, I recognize the vital importance of the worship leader and how worship is conducted. Kennon Callahan properly observes that the warmth and winsomeness of worship "has more to do with the manner in which the service is led than it does with the order of service itself."[1]

My point is that there is a shape and pattern to worship that facilitates what we are about on Sunday morning. It fits. And, I think, endures well. This ancient shape of Christian worship is described and illustrated in *Thankful Praise*, edited by Keith Watkins.[2] As one who has led several congregations in rethinking their worship in the light of this tradition, I want to share with you how we shaped it to fit our Sunday Disciples use.

Grace Shines Through Every Portion of Worship

To my mind, one of the most fascinating aspects of Alexander Campbell's thought is his conviction that every part of Lord's Day worship conveys something of God's grace. God has instituted each part of corporate worship to serve as a means of grace.

All of these ordinances, said Campbell, "proclaim some aspect of the gospel."[3] They convey something of God's grace. They are the means by which Christians enjoy God's salvation. This is so, Campbell said, "because all the wisdom, power, love, mercy, compassion, or grace of God is in the ordinances of the Kingdom of Heaven; and if all grace be in them it can only be enjoyed through them."[4] These parts of worship are the means, then, by which Christians receive God's wisdom, power, love, mercy, and compassion.

Alexander Campbell had a remarkable understanding of what happens in Lord's Day worship. In this connection he suggested a beautiful image of a congregation's Lord's Day worship. "Every part of worship," he suggested, is like a candlestick. The whole service of worship is "like so many candlesticks in a large edifice...designed to enlighten and convert the world."[5] Each part of worship is like one candle being lit until at the climax the worshiping congregation is flooded with God's light.

Shaping and Ordering Disciples Worship Today

It is helpful in examining a congregation's order of worship to keep in mind that imagery suggested by Alexander Campbell of each portion of worship uniquely conveying God's own grace. Think of a candle being lit each time we move to another action of worship until at the end the sanctuary is ablaze with the light of many candles. The test of each part of worship is whether or not one of God's graceful candles gets lit by what we are doing.

It is imperative to begin, I believe, with a clear understanding that the very nature of Sunday public worship is communal. It is the community of Christ that gathers. Worship is not a collection of isolated individuals, each indifferent to those about them. It is the worship of God's people. The church is the people of God in the company of Christ.

It is worth noting that "the breaking of bread"—Campbell's favorite term for the Lord's Supper—has a social meaning. You break bread with one another. The word *companionship* comes from two Latin words: *cum* (with) + *panis* (bread). Companionship is "breading together." It creates a bond.

So worship is Christ's community at worship. Steeped in rugged individualism as we are today, we need to be reminded of the communal nature of worship just as Campbell warned the pioneering individualists of his day. Worship is the action of community.

For purposes of clarity, worship can be characterized in four actions: (1) The Community Gathers Before God; (2) The Community Hears and Proclaims God's Word; (3) The Community Shares in Christ's Life; (4) The Community Departs for Ministry.

The Community Gathers Before God

First, *The Community Gathers Before God*. This reminds us that as we come to church we are getting back in touch with the community. Having been apart for a time, we need to re-form that community. That happens as we get out of the car and greet others. It continues as we move into a gathering room before moving on into the sanctuary. It continues in the sanctuary.

As the worshipers come together within the sanctuary, the organist may play music appropriate for persons gathering as a community for a festal occasion. We may call this a **prelude**. More accurately, it is known musically as a **voluntary**. I think the music lights a candle if it facilitates the community in reuniting for festal worship.

As the community gathers, it is appropriate to share **announcements, joys, and concerns of the people**. Such concerns are not secondary to worship but are of its substance. This sharing is the community gathered to worship and really caring about its life and the lives of one another. This is an informal but dignified period. Is there grace here? I would say a number of candles are likely to be lit during this time.

Generally, the congregation needs some time to meditate as the community moves more directly to center its thoughts upon God. The organist plays music in a more meditative mood, leading to the **call to worship**.

The call to worship may be spoken or chorally sung. It could be a brief responsive reading. In any case, its one purpose is to call the community to center upon God. In one form or another it is saying simply and directly, "Let us worship God." It is not the occasion for a familiar "Good morning" or a confession to God that we gather as sleepy-eyed people unsure of why we are here. The purpose of the call to worship is to turn the God switch on, to put it crassly. It is an effort to channel the attention of the congregation toward God. The candle only is lit here if the congregation centers upon the source of grace: God as known to us in Jesus Christ.

Then the congregation becomes more of a community as persons of all ages and conditions join together in singing a **hymn**. That in itself is an act of building the solidarity of the people of God. The words, the tune, and the action of the congregation in singing all share in upbuilding the community centered upon God.

Since the whole worship service is influenced by sharing in the Lord's Supper, this opening hymn could well express the congregation's gathering to share in word and sacrament. Contemporary hymn writers such as Brian Wren are expressing this in remarkably fresh ways.

Following the hymn there will be a **prayer**. Its purpose is still to enable the people to be a community centered upon God. Variations from week to week are helpful. There may be unison reading or responsive reading.

Sometimes the prayer may take the form of a **confession of sins**. If this is done, the worship leader may pronounce a scriptural **assurance of forgiveness**. Generally worshipers do not take kindly to reciting their sins from a written script someone else has prepared. Yet, when the words are truly reflective of its sense of guilt, a congregation may see this as fully appropriate. It may be noted that the church for its first thousand years had no place in its worship for public confession of sin.

While still standing, I have found this brief spoken **responsive** uplifting: *Minister:* "O Lord, open our mouths." *Community:* "And we shall sing your praise." Then the congregation bursts forth with the singing of the **Gloria Patri** or some other appropriate song of acclamation.

If the prayer is a confession of sin, then following the words of assurance, the responsive may be prefaced by: *Minister:* "O Lord, open our hearts," with the *Community* responding: "And we shall accept your forgiveness." Then follows the regular responsive, leading into the *Gloria Patri*. A candle is lit at this point when the congregation is facilitated in sensing a oneness in its acclamation of God.

This section of worship comes to a climax in the **pastoral prayer**. It is commonly introduced by the brief and ancient **call to prayer**: *Minister:* "The Lord be with you." *Community:* "And also with you." The pastoral prayer may take several forms, but its function is for the representative minister—the pastor of the flock—to lead in the community's praying to God. The prayer may be a **litany** in which the congregation affirms the petitions. (A litany has been described as a responsive reading in which the leader gets all the good lines to say.) It may be a **bidding prayer** of directing the congregation to pray in silence upon various topics. More commonly, it is the pastor collecting together, in a way that represents the thoughts of the community, a prayer to God. In this first section, the pastoral prayer is saying to God, "Yes, we are here, and we are together, and we are centering our lives upon you in all our frail ties, our gratitude, our yearnings and aspirations." Of course, before God, the concerns include the broader concerns of church and society.

A candle is lit at this point if something of the tough grace of God shines through. Authenticity is the key word here. The words offered to God must authentically reflect the true feelings, fears, guilt, exasperations, laments, hopes, thanksgivings of the people. Those offered words must authentically represent the nature of the God made known to us in Jesus Christ.

We should note that this pastoral prayer in some ancient traditions comes later than this, either before or after the Lord's Supper. *Thankful Praise* includes the pastoral prayer as an expression of the community's response to God. There is a tradition that this prayer is a part of our offering to God as we partake of communion. It is placed here sometimes with the explanation that we do not know how properly to pray until we have heard God's word proclaimed. In reality, that seems a bit artificial to me. The concerns of the pastoral prayer are not that directly tied up in the particular word of the Lord heard and proclaimed on any one Sunday.

I think we need to remain open to learning from early church tradition concerning the place of the pastoral prayer. Clearly it should not break up the continuity of scripture and sermon. It either comes early, as I suggest, or after the sermon or even later, after communion. As I have tried moving it around, the pastoral prayer seems an awkward break in the flow of the service everywhere but in this earlier position.

The Community Hears and Proclaims God's Word

The second main theme of worship is *The Community Hears and Proclaims God's Word.* Following the *Common Lectionary,* three **lessons** would be read: Hebrew scripture, epistles or The Acts of the Apostles, and Gospel. In sequence, the Gospel is usually read last, and in the early church tradition the congregation stood in attention to these words that most closely put us in touch with the actual words of Jesus speaking to us today. The scripture

..adings can be interspersed with an **anthem** and/or **Psalm** sung or chanted.

Traditionally, the Bible has been regarded as the book of the people. In the Roman Catholic tradition, a layperson may bring the Bible into the sanctuary as a part of the procession. In Protestant tradition, it is common for lay members to read these lessons. Alexander Campbell would agree, except he would insist that it should always be an excellent reader who knows how to express the sense of what is being read.

Our worship needs times of **silence**. It is particularly appropriate that a congregation observe a period of silence following a scripture reading. Such silence is not a blank emptiness. Rather, such silence denotes an attitude of "receptivity, of calm, of plenitude."[6] Like Mary, we take time to ponder all these things in our hearts. Silence can be indicated in the printed order of worship. In addition, the reader of scripture may convey this sign of silence by visibly folding one's hands and bowing one's head. In allowing for pregnant pauses in worship, the pauses need to come regularly in the same places each week, be ample, but consistent in length.

Both the ordering of the service and the preacher's content should make it clear that the **sermon** comes from reflecting upon the scripture. Note that God's word is heard through the reading of the scripture *and* the sermon. God's word is proclaimed in both the reading of the scripture and in the sermon.

The minister in sermon exhibits both the hearing of God's word in scripture and the proclaiming in a relevant way what has been heard. The preacher represents a responsible reading and proclaiming of God's word.

Candles are lit in this section when there is a sense that somehow through scripture and sermon a voice not our own, but that of God, has been proclaimed and heard. It is not hard to recognize those Sundays when the lights go on all over the place as the community is illumined by God's word.

In our evangelical tradition it is appropriate for an **invitation to discipleship** to follow the hearing and proclaiming of God's word. This is a particularly appropriate place to incorporate new members before moving attention to the table fellowship of the Lord's Supper. Here a hymn expressing an appropriate response to the particular message of the day may be used. If worship moves directly to the Lord's Supper, this hymn can facilitate that transition.

Traditionally, an **affirmation of faith** makes the transition from spoken word to enacted word in the Lord's Supper. Disciples have been uneasy with recitation of creeds because of their use as a test of fellowship for gathering about Christ's Table.

I am convinced that an affirmation such as the Apostles Creed is useful in reminding us all of something of the basic God-story of our faith. Creeds since the very early days of Hebrew history have generally expressed God's actions in history. I do not see the Disciples Preamble serving this function. It describes more what Disciples do than what God does. To my mind, we Disciples are much more willing to sing a creedal statement than recite it. A strong hymn of affirmation of the God-story can serve much the same purpose.

The Community Shares in Christ's Life

We move now to the third section, *The Community Shares in Christ's Life*. The title emphasizes the personal fellowship of the community with the living Christ.

The **Lord's Supper** is in the biblical tradition of symbolic action. We Disciples have emphasized the symbolic nature of bread and cup. We have sometimes missed the power that is in the doing of something symbolically. The observance of the Lord's Supper is the community's acting out the gospel symbolically.

When we read Jesus' words instituting the Lord's Supper, we note that Jesus says, "Do this in remembrance of me." There are four actions that Jesus commands:

1. Take the bread and cup.
2. Give thanks over bread and cup.

3. Break the bread.
4. Eat and drink.

All of this is symbolic action by the congregation done in remembrance of the significance of Jesus—enacting the self-giving sacrifice of Jesus Christ who through his brokenness makes us whole. The Roman Catholics teach that this sacrifice is literally made afresh by Christ each time the Lord's Supper is enacted. We Protestants see God's abounding love freshly poured out each time we liturgically reenact that sacrifice.

The worship of God is not a head trip of scintillating ideas, but the offering up of our whole beings to God in spiritual sacrifice. We freshly appropriate God's grace in Jesus Christ through taking and praying and breaking and partaking—bodily action that symbolizes the gospel in a way that no amount of words spoken can convey.

Do we not see this symbolic action at a wedding in the giving and receiving of rings? Vows are spoken, but the actions centering upon the rings have a powerful symbolism in themselves. Actions are taken that bespeak aspects of love, which at best are only stumblingly expressed in words.

Just as the exchanging of rings is an action cementing relationships, so the actions of the Lord's Supper bind those sharing in this meal more closely with one another and with our common Lord. This is a family ritual, in the best sense of the word, which not only reminds us of our relationships, but is a part of that relationship itself. It is of the substance of who we are as a community of faith. As we take these actions, we become more a part of the family centered upon the living Christ.

Therefore, the actions need to be clear. The bread and cup need to be taken up in symbolic action by the one presiding. The prayer or prayers of thanksgiving need to be grateful expressions of the gospel denoting the symbolic action. A real loaf of bread should be held up and actually broken. Alexander Campbell insisted upon real bread and a real breaking. And there needs to be active receiving.

This may be accomplished by receiving the elements in the pew as it is passed. There is strength in a congregation rising to its feet and going forward in order to partake. We are not passive recipients but active disciples claiming the gospel as ours by our bodily actions.

Traditionally, the **offering** is a part of the first action of communion. The ancient custom was to designate lay-persons to furnish the bread and the wine for a service by actually placing these elements on the table as this first action. In our Protestant tradition, the offering can be received and presented at this point as a sign of the congregation's self-giving in preparation for receiving the bread and wine. It is appropriate for the bread and wine to be symbolically placed on the table when the offering plates are received.

It is particularly appropriate for a choir's **anthem** to be sung as a part of the offertory. For the most part, the duty of the choir is to support and encourage the congregation in its worship. The choir should never substitute for the congregation's active involvement in worship. However, there is a place for trained voices to make an offering of their special gifts directly to the Lord. The anthem does not substitute for the congregation but *represents* the congregation in an artful lifting up of voices to God. The appropriate response of the congregation to such music is, silently or spoken, an Amen—not applause. It is an expression of the first action.

There are, then, in this section of the worship service, four dramatic actions—the same four Jesus took at Emmaus—"When he was at table with them, he *took* the bread and *blessed*, and *broke* it, and *gave* it to them" (Luke 24:30, RSV).

Mindful of Campbell's imagery, a great Christ candle-stick is lit when, through the congregation's actions, wor-shipers make Christ's gospel their own and meet their Savior afresh at his table.

The ancient tradition provides for the praying of the **Lord's Prayer** at the time of communion. An elder can lead the congregation in praying it as the elder concludes the prayer of thanks. This is not an easy prayer to pray and should not be casually spoken as a part of "the preliminaries" early in the service like singing the "National Anthem" before a football game. Possibly it is only as we freshly reconsecrate ourselves at Christ's Table that we can earnestly pray the Lord's Prayer. Rather than the Lord's Prayer being a routine matter, a candle of grace is lit when it is prayed thoughtfully before receiving the elements of Christ's forgiving love.

Sometimes a congregation praying the Lord's Prayer breaks into confusion, some members saying "debts" and others "trespasses." Despite the persistent variation through the ages, there is little emotional attachment to one or the other. A recent ecumenical version adopted by many church bodies suggests: "Forgive us our sins as we forgive those who sin against us."[7] Many are finding it a simple matter, while retaining the traditional language of the prayer, to indicate in the order of worship the saying of "sins." To my mind this is a helpful clarification of what the prayer means.

The Community Departs for Ministry

We come to the fourth and last portion of the service, *The Community Departs for Ministry.* The service needs to close quickly as this grand climax of worship through symbolic action is completed. There may be a brief **post-communion prayer.** To my mind, the **closing hymn** serves to express this affirmation much better as the community sings it rather than its being spoken either by one person or even in unison. Why do some people think that a unison prayer is more meaningful than that prayer being congregationally sung? The need is for a festal expression from glad hearts.

Rather quickly, the service may close with a **responsive dismissal** centering upon serving God in daily life. A **benediction** pronounced by the minister is an asking of God's blessing as the congregation departs. The benediction may be done with eyes open and heads unbowed if desired. The lifting up of hands outstretched to the congregation is an ancient Hebrew symbol of God's presence reaching out to every member.

The **closing organ selection** should be festal in mood, reflecting the spirit of moving out from the sanctuary renewed to live for Christ in the world. Someone has observed that congregations have the most trouble in Sunday public worship with how to start and how to stop. Traditions begin to build and accretions are added at these points. I am for a clean direct opening and closing. Our most recent move toward sentimental closings with a congregational chorus blow out more candles than they light.

Concluding Thoughts

This, then, is something of the way some Disciples congregations are moving toward reshaping and expressing afresh their Sunday worship. The outline is sturdy and has grace and movement to the great climax of the Lord's Supper. Worship is revitalized not by changing the worship structure each week nor by altering all the words. As Don Sailers points out, "The enabling factor in worship is a sense of being 'at home' with the forms and the language in such a way as to say and mean the words with spontaneity and conviction."[8]

Having a strong skeleton for worship, the actual worship can be expressed in various ways. Probably no form of worship has been as diversely expressed as the Roman Catholic Mass, which always has the same structure. It has been done in jazz, rock, great pomp, utter simplicity, even meaningfully with a variety of cultural expressions all in the same service. I think a pattern coming to us from the early church can serve us in a like manner.

This ancient shape and order of worship does not require a cold formality. It may result in what Horace Allen has described as a "structured informality, in contrast to what has characterized much of Protestantism: a formalized dis-order."[9] And it allows for the involvement of all the senses—more than just hearing.

What confronts the church ever and again is how best to express its worship. Or, as Alexander Campbell suggests, What can happen in Sunday worship to enable the congregation to participate in each and every part, so that one candle is lit, and another and another, till at the close the whole community is aglow with the light of God's grace?

Notes:

[1]Kennon L. Callahan, *Twelve Keys to a Successful Church* (San Francisco: Harper & Row, 1983), p. 27.

[2]Keith Watkins, ed., *Thankful Praise* (St. Louis, CBP Press, 1987).

[3]*The Christian System*, p. 184.

[4]*Ibid.*, p. 186.

[5]*Ibid.*, p. 169.

[6]J.J. von Allmen, *Worship: Its Theology and Practice*, p. 92f.

[7]International Consultation on English Texts.

[8]Don E. Sailers, "The Crisis in the Use of Language in Worship," *Music Ministry*, January 1970, p. 5.

[9]Horace T. Allen, Jr., "Is There an Emerging Ecumenical Consensus Concerning the Liturgy?" *Reformed Liturgy and Music*, Spring 1976, p. 16.

5

Singing Our Worship

Our Disciples forebears regarded congregational singing as an ordinance of Christ—a means of God's grace for the worshiper. Alexander Campbell declared, "We are divinely commanded to teach and admonish one another in psalms, hymns, and spiritual songs—to sing with grateful hearts, thus making melody in the ears of the Lord of hosts."[1]

Holding fast to his understanding of the nature of divine ordinances, Campbell stated that "the object of sacred song is to raise and exalt our spirits by divine contemplations to the sublime in the worship of our adorable God and Father."[2] As in all aspects of worship, congregational song centers upon God in adoration and is a means by which God's grace works to transform the lives of those who sing.

Alexander Campbell was the dominant publisher of hymns for his frontier religious movement. Beginning in 1828, he published a hymnal scripturally titled *Psalms, Hymns and Spiritual Songs*—the forerunner of some forty-five different editions issuing in a larger selection of hymns.[3]

Conflicting Views About Hymns

In truth, the various leaders of this movement were not of one mind about how hymns should be selected and sung. Indeed, in regard to church music, their judgments sometimes were harsh toward one another.

Alexander Campbell asserted that the standard of taste is, as he put it, "not rhyme, but reason—not the poetic feet nor the gingle of words, but the language, the sentiment, and the spiritual sense of the composition." He insisted that the "divine truth communicated in the sacred scriptures should never be sacrificed to the charms of poetry or obscured by the ornament of style."[4] Campbell encouraged a person not to sing a verse disliked and freely to modify or change any words to individual taste.

Apparently Alexander was much like his father, Thomas, who, standing as a guest in the pulpit of a church in Pittsburgh, rebuked the congregation for having the best singers sitting together with a leader and reading musical notes in worship. He counseled "that if a brother or sister found the tune pitched too high, why just pitch it a little lower. Let every one pitch it to suit himself. He saw no necessity for one tune for the whole church, and he thought that every one could sing his own tune, altering the words to whatever sound would best express the worship of the heart." A witness to this diatribe adds that Thomas Campbell "practiced what he taught."[5]

Walter Scott, an accomplished flutist, agreed with the Campbells that congregational singing is an ordinance of Christ, but drew strikingly different conclusions.

Scott, in the preface to a hymnbook he published in 1839, insisted: "It is the office of a hymn to arouse impassioned devotional feeling, even as it is the office of teaching to illuminate understanding." He observed that since congregational singing gives comfort to the aged and encouragement in the faith to youth, sacred music should "be cultivated with extraordinary care."[6]

Scott argued that if the Lord ordered his faithful to sing, then it was incumbent upon them to learn how—to the best of their abilities. Contrary to the Campbells' judgment, he encouraged participation in singing schools.

Another of these reformers, Barton W. Stone, cast yet another light upon the understanding of the place of congregational singing within a congregation. As a young pastor in Kentucky, Stone shared in a camp meeting at Cane Ridge, Kentucky, in 1801 that colored his religious understanding for life.

This Cane Ridge meeting, attended by thousands, became a spontaneous revival that cut across denominational lines. In later life, Stone recalled with amazement that, as he said: "We all engaged in singing the same songs of praise—all united in prayer—all preached these same things—free salvation urged upon all by faith and repentance."[7] He remarked how in moments of high religious excitement some individuals "in a very happy state of mind would sing most melodiously, not from the mouth or nose, but entirely in the breast."[8]

Caught up in this Cane Ridge experience, Stone composed three hymns that were widely used in his day. The camp meeting experience of revival spread rapidly. Out of those meetings sprang camp meeting spirituals—rough and rowdy, with what some derisively called their "hippity-skippity" choruses. Camp meeting spirituals became extremely popular, spreading within a short span of five years from Kentucky to the northeast.[9] Stone believed they had a place in Lord's Day worship.

In drawing to a close this quick survey of sacred music on the Disciples frontier, it should be noted that no musical instrument was used in worship "until the early 1850s at the earliest."[10] The break with those refusing to use instrumental music was yet to take place. However, Alexander

Campbell's comment on the subject would echo for a long
time. He said that "to all spiritually-minded Christians,
such aids would be as a cow bell in a concert."[11] This
movement for Christian unity was destined to split over
the use of instrumental music in worship. The non-instru-
mentalist churches congealed into the Churches of Christ
by 1910.

Today there is no editorial position or journalistic
controversy concerning Disciples church music. Yet the
issues remain, often unresolved, within our congregations. How does our Disciples faith and heritage give
guidance concerning sacred music in the contemporary
church? It is to this question that we now turn.

Hymns as a Means of Grace

To my mind, the fundamental guiding principles for
Disciples lie within Alexander Campbell's insight that
every ordered part of worship is a means of grace for the
Christian community. Worship consists of a number of
"ordinances of grace," each of which has its "own means of
development and enjoyment." Each ordinance is the means
"of a special grace peculiar to itself; so that no one can be
substituted for another, or neglected, without the lack, or
loss, of the blessing in the Divine will and Grace connected
with it."[12]

Sunday public worship is both an expression of God's
grace and the means by which believers receive it. In and
through these ordinances worshipers come to know "all
the wisdom, power, love, mercy, compassion, or GRACE
OF GOD."[13] As has been noted, Campbell expressed it
more graphically when he likened worship to the lighting
of a series of candlesticks till the room is filled with light.

So it is, then, that sacred music is an ordinance and a
means of grace. The ordinance is this, found in Colossians
3:16: "Let the word of Christ dwell in you richly in all
wisdom; teaching and admonishing one another in psalms
and hymns and spiritual songs, singing with grace in your
hearts to the Lord" (KJV). The Ephesians letter contains
the same ordinance, giving its own coloration: "Be filled

with the Spirit, as you sing psalms and hymns and spiritual songs among yourselves, singing and making melody to the Lord in your hearts" (Ephesians 5:18–19).

Colossians speaks of "singing with *grace* in your hearts"; Ephesians speaks of "singing and *making melody* in your hearts." "Making melody" is much like "singing with grace" in your hearts.

Congregational song is a means of grace. Through it worshipers experience the grace of God. Congregational singing in worship, then, must be shaped and tested in terms of its being a means of grace. As all worship, congregational song glorifies God and is reflexive in assisting Christians to grow in grace.

From this perspective, it is clear that congregational singing is an essential part of public worship. It is an apostolically ordained aspect of corporate worship through which God in gracious love comes and touches those who worship. Grace is God's self-giving. God's self is communicated to the worshiper through the congregation's singing.

This means that congregational singing is not icing on the cake—an added decoration to worship. It is not done as a warm-up leading to worship. Singing within the congregation is worship. Through it God is glorified and God works to engrave God's image upon those who sing.

The ultimate question concerning the singing of hymns in public worship is how they can best serve the congregation so as to glorify God and reflexively transmit God's abounding love in life-transforming ways. Looking at sacred music from this perspective, what do we see?

If hymn singing is a unique means of grace for the congregation, then more than casual attention needs to be paid to hymn selection, the congregation's wholehearted participation, and the singing itself. It is a matter of life in Christ.

Most attempts to define a hymn fail. Usually some one aspect of a hymn's value is emphasized to the exclusion of other aspects. In the Disciples tradition, hymns are more likely defined in a scripturally functional sense. Let me suggest that a hymn is that which is sung by a worshiping congregation—scripturally designated as a psalm, a hymn, or a spiritual song—which serves to honor God and reflexively, through the Holy Spirit, mirrors God back into the lives of the people.

There is no particular merit in trying to draw fine distinctions among psalms, hymns, and spiritual songs. Alexander Campbell, in early revisions of his hymnbook, dropped the effort to categorize songs of worship this way. Today New Testament scholars do not agree upon the precise meaning of each of these terms. All three kinds of songs have apostolic blessing for expressing worship and are regarded as ways God comes to touch those who worship.

Of course, congregational singing of hymns in worship is not so much an order to be obeyed as it is an inevitable expression of being a Christian. Martin Luther said that God has made our hearts happy through the death and resurrection of Christ, and anyone who knows this cannot help but sing about it.

Paul Westermeyer observes that "Christians are driven by an inner compulsion to sing hymns."[14] When reformers have sought to ban or limit the singing of hymns, he says, "even then the song is always latent and waiting to burst forth in a new reformation. A church that stops singing probably ceases to exist, and then one senses the rocks themselves have to cry out."[15] Westermeyer continues: "Wherever and whenever it occurs—in catacombs, houses, field, cathedrals, country churches, city churches, chapels—hymnody accompanies Christian worship. Whenever and wherever the church gathers for Word and Sacrament, whenever and wherever it gathers for the Office Hours or prayer services or preaching services or healing services, it inevitably sings hymns. Note that it *sings* hymns."[16]

Hymns Belong to the People

It is clear from scripture that hymns belong to the people—the people of God. They are not the property of the minister or the minister of music or elders or the worship committee, but of the worshipers. There is a sense in which I would describe hymns as folk songs. Possibly more accurately, they are "the ballads of the faithful."[17] They belong uniquely to the people of God as an integral part of their corporate worship. There is a right of ownership by the people. That, under God, must be taken quite seriously.

Paul Westermeyer, affirming this ownership, spells out what this implies. He says: "If a hymn is the property of the people, it must give expression to their faith, hope, aspirations, needs, ethical struggles, societal concerns, life. If it is part of the big plot of God's dealing with humanity, it must give faithful expression to what God has done in Israel, Christ, and the church and continues to do. Both relevance to the people and to the big story must be present if a hymn is to take more than the superficial shape of a hymn."[18] Hymns must be faithful to the whole scriptural God-story and expressed in words and music that are faithful to who the worshipers are.

The words, of course, are important. They must express true faith and genuine religious sentiment. However, those who select hymns need to keep in mind that members of the congregation vary widely as to how they express their faith in words. Many are not theologically sophisticated and are satisfied in knowing that Christ died on a cross for them and was raised in triumph from the dead. They do not worry much about which doctrine of the atonement is correct and the details of Christ's resurrection. They may find nothing contradictory in singing conflicting theological formulations. In this they reflect the New Testament itself, which comfortably sets forth varying theological interpretations—all regarded as worthy of normative expression.

The scriptures express the Christian faith and its doctrines through a variety of images. So may the hymns of Christian worship. It is exceedingly important to keep in mind that hymns are not composed to be recited but to be sung. Hymns serve as a means to worship God, through the Christ, in the Spirit. They also serve as a means of God's self-giving grace in reflexive action back into the lives of those who sing. The fact that the hymn is sung helps to shape how it is expressed in words.

Therefore, a hymn is not necessarily a poem put to music—a poem that must stand on its own literary merits apart from its singing. The only reality that a hymn has is when it is sung. The words and style of expression will reflect more that of the congregation's liturgy—its spoken ways of worshiping—than be in themselves great literature. Like good folk songs, hymns for congregational singing will for the most part express basic metaphors of life such as light, darkness, birth, death, height, depth. They will reflect the central biblical images of Christian faith. The words of hymns walk a fine line between being, on the one hand, too metaphorically elaborate to be easily grasped or expressed by the singer, and on the other, being so barren of all imagery that they are dull and boring.

In reality, the good hymns are governed by poetic restraint. That remarkable composer of hymns, Isaac Watts, confessed that the most difficult thing about writing hymns was "suppressing the muse." Contemporary composer of hymns, Gracia Grindal, in quoting Watts, adds, "Hymns are poems, the most difficult and restrained poems one can write."[19]

One aspect of hymns that makes them "difficult" is that they must convey clear meaning the first time sung, and yet they must have sufficient artistic merit to convey fresh meaning as they are sung repeatedly over the years. The words of hymns may well express the Christian faith and experience in ways that would not normally occur to the individual singer. They may articulate what the singer is yearning to express. As a contemporary hymn writer, Brian Wren has put it in a bit of verse, a hymn may elicit from the singers some such thought as this:

Yes!
that's what I mean, though I couldn't have said it;
that's what I believe, though I couldn't express it;
that's how I feel, though I couldn't explain it;
that's true for me, though it wasn't till I read it.[20]

The Crucial Importance of Tune

Fundamentally, however, a hymn is unique in the sense that it is intended for singing. There is a sense in which the music of a hymn is more important than the words. The uniqueness of a hymn does not lie in its literary quality but in the fact that the words are sung to music. Music is a means of expressing feeling. It is capable of stirring deep emotions.

Much of the feeling tone in worship comes from sacred music sung and played. Music cannot in itself convey ideas, but it can, when wedded properly to thought, assist a congregation in expressing its faith with feeling. When Disciples worship is heavily weighed toward the rational, it is all the more important that the music give emotional balance. Of course, the music must fit the mood of the words. Neither the words nor the tunes of hymns should be sentimental—exaggerated thought and feeling. When honest words are sung with appropriate music, "ideas are charged with power."[21]

This is why congregational singing of hymns is not optional to worship. It is a means of expressing one's faith with feeling. It is, as Alexander Campbell insisted, an ordinance of worship. The singing of hymns is a means of enjoying God's presence and receiving God's abounding grace. The hymn, then, has failed to do what it was intended to do if it is not sung by the congregation. There is an ancient argument within the church as to whether in selecting hymns the words or the tune should be the primary consideration. Often clergy and musicians, congregation and pastor, polarize around this issue.

I think we can learn from the congregation about what hymns are for. Worshipers think it is rather basic to hymns that they be sung. They are properly disturbed when they cannot sing the tunes. We know that "many of the favorite hymns of our congregations have become so because of the tunes; that is, because they are easy and enjoyable to sing." D. Darrell Woomer, making this observation, goes on to add: "Only after many years of association of tune and text do the words become important. Similarly many of the new

hymn texts are accepted or rejected because of the music
that accompanies them. For most congregations, the music comes first, for if they like the tune then the text will be
accepted."²² Woomer concludes that "hymns are chosen
because of the words and congregations sing them because
of the tune."

Instinctively, a congregation knows that a hymn is not
a hymn until it is sung. Common sense tells worshipers
that those words on the page cannot be a hymn for them
unless they can sing it. Just as a bell is not a bell until it
is rung, so a hymn is not a hymn until it is sung.

There is, of course, some truth in this, but why are we
so defensive at times about the unfamiliar tunes we
choose? Hymns are not theology to recite; they are faith
and experience to be sung. The singing is not secondary to hymn selection, but crucial. If the hymns are not
heartily sung, then the words do not accomplish their
intention. In some sense our worship has failed. No
candle of God's grace is lit. The ordinance has not been
fulfilled.

Of course, the matching of tune and words is vitally
important. The tune must be singable and memorable. It
must be a tune that the congregation owns and wants to
sing. A tune is not a bit of medicine, which, though hard to
swallow, is nevertheless good for you. Erik Routley has
observed that "for 90 percent the pleasure of singing
hymns is bound up with their music."²³ Routley also
observed that "hymns are songs for unmusical people to
sing together."²⁴ The truth is that, as James Rawlings
Sydnor has said, "The average congregation probably has
a majority of people who would say that they 'couldn't
carry a tune in a bucket.'"²⁵

The selecting of a hymn tune is not an afterthought.
Artistically, the tune needs to support the hymn's mood
and expression. But it is not the right tune if the congregation does not sing it. We shall keep our heads about
hymn singing if we bear in mind the ordinance given to us
in Colossians: "Let the word of Christ dwell in you richly;
teach and admonish one another in all wisdom; and with

gratitude in your hearts sing psalms, hymns, and spiritual songs to God" (Colossians 3:16).

The Corporate Nature of Hymn Singing

There is a social or corporate aspect to hymn singing. Congregational singing serves not only in "singing with grace in your hearts to the Lord," but in addressing one another. The congregational singing of hymns unifies and strengthens the sense of community and fellowship among the members.

We know by experience that convening a group of Christians by singing a hymn assists that group in sensing its oneness. Something of the grace of God that comes to us through congregational singing is the increasing sense of relating more closely to one another. Congregational singing builds community. That is not a secondary aspect of hymn singing. It is another illustration of how our worship is reflexive. Even as we center our common song in Christ, the Holy Spirit comes among us in grace-giving ways. We are bound more closely to one another in our singing of hymns.

In the late fourth century, John Chrysostom, bishop of Constantinople, said this in a sermon after hearing the congregation sing a Psalm: "The psalm which occurred just now in the office blended all voices together, and caused one single fully harmonious chant to arise; young and old, rich and poor, women and men, slaves and free, all sang one single melody....All the fine qualities of social life are here banished. Together we make up a single choir in perfect equality of right and of expression where by earth imitates heaven. Such is the noble character of the Church."[26] Such, we might add, is the noble character of congregational song.

Hymns, then, as a holy ordinance for the church, must not only be theologically sound but heartily sung by the congregation. The grace does not come until the words and notes of music printed in a hymnal fly off the page and take wing in congregational song.

The truth is that congregational singing in many congregations can hardly be described as grace-giving.

Though intended as means of grace, they seem not to breathe the breath of life. Renewal of congregational singing of hymns is urgent.

The singing of each hymn in worship contains its own unique gift of God's grace. As congregations heartily sing, it is like the lighting of a series of candles, till at the close the sanctuary is full of God's bright light. The members of the congregation go out into the world not only illuminated, but strangely warmed by the glow of the living Christ within their hearts.

Notes

[1]*The Millennial Harbinger*, New Series, VI (1842), 5, p. 231.

[2]*The Christian Baptist*, p. 406.

[3]Claude E. Spencer, "The Campbell Hymn Book," *Discipliana*, VIII (1950), January, p. 47.

[4]*The Millennial Harbinger*, New Series, VII (1843), 3, pp. 129-130.

[5]J. S. Lamar, *Memoirs of Isaac Errett* (Cincinnati: Standard Publishing Company, 1893), II, p. 25f., footnote.

[6]Charles Huddleston Heaton, "The Disciples of Christ and Sacred Music," doctoral dissertation submitted to Union Theological Seminary, June 2, 1956, p. 72f.

[7]John Rogers, *Biography of Elder Barton W. Stone*, p. 37f.

[8]*Ibid.*, pp. 40-42.

[9]Richard Huffman Hulan, "Cane Ridge and the Music It Propelled," *The Hymn*, October 1984, p. 199ff.

[10]Walter M. Sikes, "Worship Among Disciples of Christ (1809-1865)," *Mid-Stream*, VII, 4 (Summer 1968), p. 27.

[11]*The Millennial Harbinger*, Fourth Series, I, 9 (1851), p. 581f.

[12]*The Millennial Harbinger*, March 1859, p. 132f.

[13]*The Christian System*, p. 186.

[14]"What Is a Hymn?" *Reformed Liturgy and Music*, Summer 1987, p. 136.

[15]*Ibid.*

[16]*Ibid.*

[17]*Ibid.*

[18]*Ibid.*

[19]"Pitfalls in Hymn Writing," *The Hymn*, April 1984, p. 82f.

[20]"The Hymn Today: The Challenge of the Words," *Hymn Society of Great Britain and Ireland Bulletin*, #138, January 1977, p. 204.

[21]S. Paul Schilling, *The Faith We Sing* (Philadelphia: Westminster, 1983), p. 36.

[22]"Selecting Hymns for Public Worship," *The Hymn*, 1983.

[23]Erik Routley, *Hymns Today and Tomorrow* (New York: Abingdon Press, 1964), p. 17.

[24]Quoted by Eric Sharpe, "Review of Thomas Troeger's 'New Hymns for the Lectionary,'" *Hymn Society of Great Britain and Ireland Bulletin*, #168, July 1986, p. 150.

[25]James Rawlings Sydnor, "How to Improve Congregational Singing," *The Hymn*, Summer 1987, p. 153.

[26]Quoted by Kathryn L. Nichols, "Music and Musician in Service of the Church," *The Hymn*, Spring 1986, p. 75.

6

Changing Some Aspects of Worship

The worship of the church has a way of changing through the years. Looking back upon our Disciples heritage of frontier worship, we recognize some continuing familiarities such as the primacy of the Lord's Supper in each Sunday service. But it was common in those times to have three services of worship on a Sunday with the Lord's Supper in a social afternoon service. We wouldn't stand for that today. We are comfortable with our forebears' insistence upon the priesthood of all believers, but we find it strange that in worship the men sat on one side of the meeting house and the women on the other. If there were slaves, they sat in the gallery.

It appears there are some fixed elements of worship that remain largely the same, but others that change with the times. The question arises as to why these shifts come and how the church deals with change.

When you think about it, changes in worship stem largely from two sources. First, the assembly of Christ's fellowship is composed of human beings who express themselves according to how they are culturally shaped. The realities of American frontier existence helped determine the way our forebears worshiped. In the beginning, Disciples were largely rural folk. When they came to the city, their ways of expressing worship began to change to reflect their new setting. Old informal ways suddenly became uncouth. Baptisms in a river with no dressing facilities had been matter-of-fact and informal. In contrast, baptizing in the sanctuary called for less sloshing of water and the quick exit of the candidate to a dressing room to "look presentable."

A second source for change in worship is the shifting of the church's self-understanding. In their early days, Disciples saw themselves as called to restore the church to its apostolic roots. While firmly holding to the oneness of the church, they at the same time believed all churches should adhere to their own self-understanding. Christian unity would come as Disciples enlightenment transformed all other church bodies. In this they became sectarian— giving the impression that everyone was wrong but them.

Over a period of time, Disciples began to recognize more clearly the authenticity of other churchly expressions. With the restructuring of the church in 1968 and the adoption of a Design, Disciples confirmed a new self-understanding. They recognized that Disciples are a people that is more than just a collection of congregations. Further, they recognized they are a people related in all times and places to Christ's one universal church. They recognized that the church's two thousand years of history is a part of who they are. The whole heritage of Christianity is a part of Disciples heritage.

With this fresh self-understanding, Disciples have begun to appropriate this rich heritage into their life of worship. So, we have begun to learn how to shape worship as we have studied the way Christians of the early formative centuries shaped their services. While continuing to witness to the values of immersion of persons old enough to claim Christ for themselves, we have recognized the validity of those who have been baptized in other ways. We have begun to grow in our sense of accountability to the universal church as to how and why we worship as we do.

Today every Disciples congregation is caught in this ferment of change. Often the very fabric of Christian community becomes tattered, if not torn, by controversy as to what changes are appropriate in the conducting of worship.

It is helpful in these circumstances to understand the dynamics of change. Some thoughtful analysis may help in deciding what to change and how to go about it.

I have already pointed out one place to begin. In looking at possible changes, sort them out as to whether they are cultural issues or matters of church identity. Somehow we should be able to be more flexible in varying our cultural expressions than in making changes that affect how we understand ourselves as a church.

Another helpful way to analyze changes in worship is to use what I call a planetary model of worship.[1] Use your imagination and think of worship as a planetary system. At the center there is the sun representing the central affirmations of the church. These are rather fixed, and though they may change in some aspects, they don't change very much or very fast.

Circling around the sun of core expressions are planetary aspects of worship that all have some relationship to the sun but give it more concrete expression. These are the essential ingredients of worship such as Campbell's ordinances of prayer, hymns, scripture, sermon, Lord's Supper, and the like. Like planets they vary in distance from the sun and have different weights, though all are vital to the planetary system. They are rather fixed in their ways but do change with time. At different points in history each has varied in regard to how each has been valued.

Each of these planetary ordinances has moons circling about it. These are the ways we express the ordinances. They have to do with degrees of formality or how we express ourselves in prayer—by bowing or kneeling or shouting Amen. They include deciding, as the Campbells remind us, whether or not we shall as a congregation all sing the same tune with the same words. They deal with such matters as the use of guitars and banners and balloons. These seem to change more easily, slipping in and out of use.

In discussing changes it can be helpful to chart the issues in terms of where they fit within the planetary system of worship. The closer to the center, the greater the difficulties and implications for change. The farther away, the more flexible the changes may be.

Yet, our planetary model of worship is a bit more complex than this. The whole system is in dynamic relation to all its parts. Changes in some of the moonlike qualities of worship can make an impact upon how the planets operate and even how aspects of the fixities of the sun are understood. In fact, it is often these peripheral aspects that sometimes have the most profound implications. Following our analogy, although the sun and planets and moons remained just the same, Copernicus introduced a whole new understanding of the planetary system that we call today the Copernican revolution. Radical shifts in the understanding of worship can take place.

There are two particularly controversial issues of worship facing contemporary Disciples. They are a source of much pain and grief on the part of countless members. It is urgent that they be resolved promptly in truth and love. One has to do with the question of the language we use in worship. The other has to do with whether or not children who have not been baptized should partake of the Lord's Supper.

Inclusive Language

There is a vital current of thought today pressing for the use of inclusive language in worship. We are becoming

increasingly aware that either inadvertently or intentionally we have excluded some persons from receiving their
full dignity in worship. The language that we use regarding persons has a powerful impact upon them—for good or
ill. Language helps shape our understanding of reality.

Christians, sensitive to the feelings of others, will not
want to use derogatory language to refer to them in
worship. Words like savage and heathen are no longer
appropriate. We are learning to speak of the impaired,
rather than the halt and the lame. We should not link
blackness to sin and whiteness to purity.

Inclusiveness has also to do with acknowledging that
children are present. Hymns, prayers, and preaching need
to reflect that children, as well as adults are bringing their
worship.

Inclusiveness has also to do with those of other cultures
and families of faith. Do the hymns used in worship reflect
the varied background of the congregation's members? Do
they express the catholicity of the church—the varied
strands of Christian expression that make up Christ's one
church? A congregation may want consciously to include in
its singing black or white spirituals, hymns composed in
Jamaica or China or South Africa.

Seeking to be inclusive in its language, a congregation
will also be concerned about the continued use of *man* and
men as generic terms for females as well as males. Whether
or not the people are crying out for change, inclusive
language is transforming our vocabulary. To be inclusive
in gender is not just a matter of opinion, but one of
justice. It is a part of our culture's discrimination against
women.

The contemporary hymn composer, Brian Wren, has
written: "As a white, male, middle-class, English Christian, I have come to see that my society is deeply male-
dominated. The questioning of sexism in language is not a
frill, an 'extra,' or a surface issue. It reflects deeper stirrings,
questioning social inequalities. Such questioning ought to
find a particularly keen interest among Christians, whose
Lord approached women in a radically different, dignity-

perceiving way from social conventions of his time, and who founded a church based on the unity and equality of free and slave, Jew and Gentile, female and male."[2] Discrimination is fostered by our sexist language in worship. We cannot get off the hook by insisting that the generic meaning of the word *man* originally meant a human person of either gender. That, of course, is true. Aelfric in about A.D. 1000 said, "His mother was a Christian named Elen, a very full-of-faith mann, and extremely pious."[3] Today the most chauvinist male would have trouble with that sentence. In other cases the words fathers and brothers were intentionally exclusive and discriminatory.

Not only our English words have changed their meaning in regard to the sexes, but our attitudes as well. We Disciples have officially amended our Design to expunge from it any reference to what we so fondly once called our "brotherhood." Continued usage of the word *brothers* as an inclusive term for brothers and sisters is out. We are children of God. The future is with sexually inclusive language.

More perplexing and disturbing is the question of being inclusive in our language when we speak of God. Our language about God has been male dominated. We are being challenged to cease and desist this practice. Thinking about it, we recognize that all of our language about God is picture-language. We speak of God in metaphors, mental and poetic images. God transcends all the pictures we try to use in description. We know that. But the question is whether or not we should abandon our references to God as male.

Some insist that male imagery of God must be abandoned. In so doing, God may be spoken of not as Father, Son, and Holy Spirit; but, rather, as Creator, Redeemer, Sustainer; or, possibly, Creator, Word, Spirit. But these do not serve as dynamic equivalents of what has traditionally been meant by these terms. Some advocate that even Christ should never be referred to as a male, saying that when Jesus arose from the dead he was taken into the Godhead, which transcends all sexuality.

Thinking about God as person is one of the most meaningful ways we have of relating to God. Did not Jesus express the intimacy we may have with God in terms of God being our loving Father? And what does it do to our picture of the Christ if we separate the risen Christ from the Jesus who walked in Galilee?

The God language we use particularly in singing hymns has become a problem. When asked, most people in the pews say they are either indifferent to the issue or opposed to any change. Nevertheless, the future lies with more inclusive ways of identifying God than our older language affords. Brian Wren observes that "these changes are going to take place and most of the important battles over this matter have already been won."[4] Denominational hymnals recently published or being published are responding positively in some manner to greater inclusivity in regard both to all human beings and to expressions for God.

The transition will not come easily and the fabric of congregations may well be torn in the process. That's a problem. But there is an opportunity here as well.

The opportunity is to grow in our understanding of the nature of human beings and of God. In the light of God's revelation in Christ we must become more inclusive in our language regarding human beings. This is a matter of justice.[5]

In regard to the God language we use, we have an opportunity to follow biblical precedent and use both male and female imagery to express who God is. Sometimes we recognize God in motherhood; sometimes in fatherhood. Recognizing that we have so overdone the male imagery of God that we have distorted our understanding of both God and our sisters, we need consciously to be more inclusive in our imagery of God. We have been warned by scripture not to worship images but the living God.

It is crucial to keep in mind, as we seek to overcome our sexist language, that we are trying our best to express who God is. Constance F. Parvey reminds us: "Inclusive language is not just a question of slotting in a few changed words here and there, a kind of religious anagram.... Theological language is the language of addressing and hearing God. It is language that probes the depths of the mystery of life—of where we have come from, go and find unique meaning for our existence....God is always Yahweh (I Am Who I Am). Only God defines God's self."[6]

In regard to the use of the trinitarian formula, Father, Son, and Holy Spirit, we face a knotty problem. This formulation is dominated by male imagery. It clearly reinforces a picture of God as exclusively male. Its heavy use increasingly feels oppressive to contemporary sensitive ears. Yet, the New Testament cannot be understood adequately in any other terms. Jesus in life and word conveyed his profoundly intimate relationship to God in terms of Father and Son. Referring to that relationship as Creator and Redeemer in no way represents the same thing.

Although the Campbells did not like the term "trinitarian," their very understanding of Christian worship was at heart trinitarian. "We worship the Father, through the Son, by the Holy Spirit." Furthermore, they insisted, as have all Christians through the ages, that a person be baptized into the name of the Father and the Son and the Holy Spirit. One enters the church baptized into that name and one gathers for worship in the name of Father, Son, and Holy Spirit.

Looking at this in the light of our planetary model of worship, we must say that the trinitarian expression concretely expressed in the three names is a core belief. It is not likely to change any time soon. At present our mutual recognition of members across all denominational lines is specifically based upon baptism with water in the name of the Father, Son, and Holy Spirit. With our Disciples understanding of the oneness of Christ's church we must not break this mutuality casually.

But the pain and the injustice remain. I believe at some point the church will find a new way to express this ancient formula or to give it a different value. In the meantime, I think congregations can prophetically begin to explore ways these changes can come.

For example, although the traditional trinitarian formula needs to be spoken over the baptismal candidate, there can be feminine allusions to God included as a part of that formula. For example, the minister may say, "As God gives birth to a newborn through the breaking of waters, so God gives you new life through the breaking of these waters as you are baptized in the name of the Father and of the Son and of the Holy Spirit." Returning to our planetary system of change in worship, the formula has been preserved but modified by the moonlike worship addition of fresh imagery.

Another creative possibility is to include Ruth Duck's remarkably sensitive reformulation of the trinitarian baptismal formula within a Disciples act of baptism. Although she offers her reformulation in place of the traditional trinitarian words, I think it could also be used together with the words of Jesus' great commission in this time of transition. The officiant could say:

> Baptizing you in the spirit of Jesus who calls us
>   to "Go, therefore and make disciples of all
>   nations, baptizing them in the name of
>   the Father and of the Son and of the Holy
>   Spirit," I ask you:
>
> Do you believe in God, the Source, the fountain of
>   life?
>
> **I believe.**
>
> Do you believe in Christ, the offspring of God,
>   embodied in Jesus of Nazareth and in the
>   church?
>
> **I believe.**
>
> Do you believe in the liberating Spirit of God, the
>   wellspring of new life?
>
> **I believe.**[7]

The candidate is then baptized. A dynamic equivalency to the traditional meaning of the trinitarian formula has thus been emphasized, while linking it with the words presently required for mutual recognition by various church bodies. It would be fully appropriate for the whole congregation to join in the responding to these questions as a reaffirmation of their baptismal faith.

There are glorias and doxologies and benedictions that use a variety of expressions for God. The greater use of these, along with a de-emphasis upon the trinitarian formula when not essential, can have long-term effects. Although in prayer, scripture, and sermon it may at times be essential to refer to Father and Son out of biblical faithfulness, many, if not most, references need not be gender specific.

These changes, initially seeming peripheral, do have their long-term effects even upon how one views the central subject of our faith. The planetary system of worship is a dynamic relation in which a change at any point effects some change in all parts.

This issue of inclusive language is a matter not of choice but of truth. A congregation needs leadership and guidance from its pastors and church musicians in becoming more inclusive. The issue of inclusive language for human beings and for God must not be indifferently shrugged off as only "one more crusade" by a few disgruntled people. More and more we find the "gruntled" asking questions as well. God's future is with an inclusive expression of the nature of God. This is a significant opportunity for our congregations to grow in the knowledge of God and one another.

Children and the Lord's Supper

Increasingly, the question is being raised as to whether it may be appropriate for children who have not formally professed their faith and been baptized to share in the meal of the Lord's Supper. Is this not a family meal where children and parents alike can share together in table fellowship? Why should children be discriminated against? Parents, aware that young children develop a trusting faith in the God of Jesus Christ long before the usual age for joining the church have a hard time explaining why these little believers should be barred from communing with the one who said, "Let the children come."

Historically, there is no question that Disciples on the frontier firmly held that only those who had professed faith in Christ and been baptized should partake of the Lord's Supper. Baptism was the prime ordinance—the first step in becoming a Christian. It was the great monumental act in which persons bodily reenacted the death, burial, and resurrection of their Lord. The Lord's Supper, signifying exactly the same thing, was the weekly monumental way of refreshing baptism's meaning. There was believers' baptism and believers' Lord's Supper.

That seemed to be a satisfactory explanation for many decades. However, with the changes of time Disciples have come to a culturally different understanding of who children are and how they develop. They have also come to a different understanding of the nature of the church. The result has been a rethinking of the role of children in the life of the church and an increased questioning of older practices.

One of the radical cultural shifts that has taken place since frontier days has to do with the expected role of the church in the Christian nurture of children. Our Disciples forebears regarded the home as the primary means of passing the faith of one generation on to the next. The family gathered regularly at home for religious devotion. Families brought their hymnbooks to church on Sunday because they had been using them at home all week. Children learned the gospel story literally at their mothers' knees.

Today this responsibility for the Christian nurture of children has been largely delegated to the church. Parents have not fully abdicated this task, but depend substantially upon the congregation to shape their children's faith. The church, with this changing self-understanding, has developed church schools, fellowships, children's sermons or children's church, and pastor's membership classes to meet this challenge.

As the church has renewed acquaintance with its children and its importance to the community, it has come to recognize that spiritual formation is not just a matter of drilling biblical facts and religious moralisms into children's heads. Children soak up influences through seeing and hearing and smelling. They grasp the faith through participation in a community of faith. One gets a feel for Christian faith and life by sharing in its festivals, singing its songs, listening as elders pray, catching and repeating its fixed prayers. A child learns reverence by experiencing reverence within a worshiping congregation. One feels one's way into faith as much as one learns through direct verbal teaching.

From this kind of perspective the question arises as to whether or not it is crucial to a child's spiritual formation to share in the central reason worshipers gather for worship on Sunday—the partaking of the Lord's Supper.

An added complexity arises in the fact that church bodies that practice infant baptism often express their inclusion of children in the family of God by allowing them to partake of the Lord's Supper before they are confirmed. With our mobile population it is common for a Disciples congregation to have within its fellowship children who have already been baptized but not yet confirmed. According to their traditions they may have already partaken of the Lord's Supper. Do we serve these children who were baptized as infants, but not those whose baptism has been delayed to a more accountable age?

The result is that with these shifts in both our understanding of children and the nature of the church, we grow less certain as to how we regard children and communion.

An approach to clarifying our understanding is to recall what in Disciples tradition the Lord's Supper is. It is monumental. The Lord's Supper is not primarily a means of maintaining discipline—barring some people from entry and inviting others to come in. It is an open table of remembrance. So it does not fit our tradition to think in terms of who legally can or cannot partake of bread and cup.

But, as a monument, the Lord's Supper conveys profound meanings. It portrays in word and deed the gospel story of Christ's life, death, burial, and resurrection to reconcile the world to God. Two thousand years of theological reflection have not plumbed the depths of what that means. One does not casually regard this monument of meaning.

Moreover, standing within this monument we come to know the living Christ, present to us in these moments as at no other time in our lives. Christ presides at the table and speaks an invitation to embrace us afresh within the fellowship of his love. One does not receive that invitation and embrace without the awesome realization of what is taking place.

Recalling my own experience with monuments, I remember as a child being taken by my mother and father to visit the Lincoln Memorial in Washington D.C. I was too small to understand the issues of the Civil War and what cares had furrowed the brow of that brooding figure of Lincoln. The one thing I remember my mother telling me was that during the war a sentry found asleep on duty had been sentenced to death, but Lincoln, having pity upon him, forgave him and sent him back to his post. That wasn't the whole story of Lincoln's greatness, but a piece of it—a real piece of the whole. I was too young to grasp the issues that caused a grateful people to erect this monument to a beloved president, but I still feel within my bones the sense of awe I experienced within that special space.

I am convinced that there must be a way for children to experience the monument of the Lord's Supper—to participate in it, to move around and sense its power. This can only happen adequately by participating at the table.

Children learn relationships of love long before they know how to articulate love's meaning. They can express love before they can formulate its implications. That is why church bodies that baptize infants are becoming more open to children receiving communion. A United Methodist bishop tells of his five-year-old granddaughter stepping forward to receive communion. When asked why she went to the Lord's Table, she replied, "To say Hi to Jesus." Few adults could put it better. The complication, a serious one, is that all other church bodies understand the Lord's Table as reserved only for ones who are baptized. This emerging consensus is expressed in the carefully wrought *Baptism, Eucharist and Ministry*—possibly the most significant ecumenical document of the twentieth century.

I believe it is appropriate for Disciples, while respecting ecumenical consensus, to develop a practice that fits our distinctive view of believer's baptism. Many of the other faith communities don't have our problems and need to understand how with integrity we seek our own solutions.

There is an ancient Latin expression, *lex orandi, lex credendi*, which means, "Let the law of prayer establish the law of belief." It is a way of saying that how the church worships defines what it believes. Faith grows out of the experience of worship. I am suggesting that Disciples develop a common way of including children in worship that will affect what we believe about the church and God.

In terms of our planetary image of worship, I see our developing a moonlike structure that may ultimately reverberate with implications far into the center of the system itself. An example of how this is done is the way the blessing or dedication of infants has developed into a common practice among Disciples. It began in the 1940s in response to a felt need to include unbaptized children into the life of the community. It was not the result of a study commission or a special authorization. Rather, it began to be practiced and congregation after congregation began to own it. The practice has in time moved from being a tentative new moon to planetary status. I see that very same rite affecting now how we regard that sun-like core practice of the Lord's Supper.

It would be possible, at the time when children are presented before the congregation in an act of thanksgiving and covenanting, to enroll them in what traditionally has been called the **catechumenate**. That term was used in the second century to designate a lengthy procedure for preparing persons for baptism. Over a period as long as three years these candidates would be gradually introduced into the various aspects of Christian worship and living.

Since the term *catechumenate* may sound foreign to Disciples congregations, another term may be preferred— **children of the covenant**. This would emphasize the communal responsibility assumed at the time of infant dedication of both the parents and the larger community of faith.

A congregation and parents could covenant rather specifically to enter into a disciplined approach to preparing these children for the time when they would profess for themselves Jesus as Lord and be baptized. The church as a part of its Christian nurture would specifically program ways for the children to experience congregational life. This would involve them inclusively in a variety of intentional ways. A part of their growing sense of inclusion would be upon special occasions to share in the Lord's Supper. Although these would be genuine experiences of communion, they would be recognized as being limited by the fuller commitment that comes with believers' baptism.

In this fashion, the matter would not be left up to parental discretion, unless parents decided they did not want their children to participate. It would not make a distinction between children who were baptized as infants and those still looking toward baptism. It would not be often. Maybe beginning once when becoming a five-year-old and then a couple of special times each year thereafter. Their readiness would depend upon their ability to sit through the entire service of worship in such a way as not to be unduly disturbing to others who worship. Even though these children may ordinarily be excused for children's church, they need on these special Sundays to participate in the whole service of worship. The actual partaking of the Lord's Supper is within the context of hearing God's word through scripture reading and preaching.

Each of these occasions would be preceded by preparation and interpretation. It would be much like getting ready to visit a monument. The children would be prepared as to how to act and what to expect and something of what is meant. All of this would be in the context of preparation for the time when one assumes full responsibility for one's life in Christ through baptism. These occasions for inclusive participation may be a noteworthy observance for the congregation as well. Through special recognition by the congregation there can be a growing bonding within this fellowship of faith of all its family.

Such an approach to children and communion is a bending, if not breaking, of the ecumenical rules. It is not casually done. It should be interpreted as the way a church that practices believers' baptism takes its responsibilities for its catechumens, or children of the covenant, with complete seriousness. It would be a Disciples way of *lex orandi, lex credendi*—allowing the way we worship to shape what the church believes.

Developing a Climate of Openness

Disciples congregations have a rich heritage of respecting diversity within their fellowship. They have not required tight adherence to a specific set of theological beliefs. They have encouraged differences of opinions. They regard their members to be competent to think through church issues in the light of apostolic heritage and come to responsible decisions.

As changes in Sunday worship are contemplated, a congregation needs to reaffirm this sacred trusting of one another. Although discussion may at times be heated, there should be no questioning the motives, the integrity, or the Christian commitment of one another. As Disciples, this is taken for granted as basic to an understanding of who church members are.

Rather, assuming the goodwill upon the part of all, there can be free discussion, an openness to consideration of a diversity of views, and a searching for what faithfulness requires in the midst of changing times. Recognizing that the Holy Spirit is not bound to any set of dogmas, but has a disconcerting way of stirring up new insights and fresh ways of thinking within the church, a congregation can embrace these controversial issues as opportunities for growth.

Each member, however persuaded of the truth, has not only a right to be heard but an obligation to speak. It is through the diversity of gifts that the church finds it way. With the full participation of all, led by the Spirit, a congregation shall know the truth that theirs is truly the worship of the people.

Notes

[1]I was stimulated to develop this model from suggestions by Thomas H. Troeger, "Personal, Cultural and Theological Influences on the Language of Hymns and Worship," *The Hymn*, October 1987, p. 7; and Edward Schillebeekx, *Jesus: An Experiment in Christology*, translated by Hubert Hoskins (New York: The Seabury Press, 1979), p. 576.

[2]Brian Wren, "Sexism in Hymn Language," *The Hymn*, October 1983, p. 229.

[3]*Ibid.*

[4]*Ibid.*

[5]Keith Watkins develops this convincingly in his book, *Faithful and Fair* (Nashville: Abingdon Press, 1981).

[6]Constance F. Parvey, "Language as Life-Bearing," *The Hymn*, October 1983, p. 235.

[7]Ruth Duck, *Gender and the Name of God: The Trinitarian Baptismal Formula* (New York: The Pilgrim Press, 1991), p. 185.

7

Owning the Service of Worship

As worship on the American frontier developed, its ministerial leaders grew in their concern for fuller participation of worshipers in their Lord's Day gatherings. It is interesting to note the common way in which our forebears began sensing something was not quite right.

Walter Scott, in 1842, returned from a three-month visit to churches east of his home in Ohio, disturbed by what he had witnessed. He found the churches generally more concerned with having the proper ordinances than in sharing in the power of their grace. He said that they "sometimes do not believe in the holy spirit's being given to believers, they sometimes do not believe in prayer, they are therefore seen at the moment of prayer standing, not kneeling, and gazing around upon all present as if they stood in a menagerie of wild beasts."[1] He observed that "while their notions of order extend to a strict attention to the ritual of Christianity, their obedience may be said to be...seen in ordinances rather than in a meek quiet spirit and a generous and loving behavior towards all saints and all men." This "standing while praying and of looking around on others on such occasions," he declared showed a great lack of devotion.

Barton W. Stone returned the next year from visiting churches in Indiana, Ohio, and Kentucky, with much the same complaint. He noted that generally at the time of partaking the Lord's Supper worshipers "seemed to attend to the ordinance as a duty, or as a custom, and not as a divine privilege—many of them sitting and gazing around on the multitude, and the passing events among them, while they were receiving the symbols of the body and blood of Christ!" He asked: "Will not the mind be carried off by the eye? Can we attend to two objects at the same time? Can we at the same time affectionately remember a dying Savior, and be attentive to surrounding objects? I think it impossible."[2]

Upon reading these accounts I was struck by their common use of the word "gaze." At the heart of the problem lay the fact that the worshipers were not really engaged in what they were about. With a "gaze" one turns from active involvement in worship to being a spectator.

Fighting Formalism

In this our forebears were touching upon the great danger of worship. For all too many persons worship becomes a routine: motions to go through, form without substance.

In our free-church tradition, Disciples sought to solve this problem by doing away with fixed prayers and liturgies. Is it not these fixed structures that stand between the worshiper and God? Religiously sensitive naturalist Annie Dillard expressed this viewpoint when she wrote: "I often think of the set pieces of liturgy as certain words which people have successfully addressed to God without their getting killed. In the high churches they saunter through the liturgy like Mohawks along a strand of scaffolding who have long since forgotten their danger. If God were to blast such a service to bits, the congregation would be, I believe, genuinely shocked."[3]

In a sense, our Disciples forebears blew such services to bits, setting congregations free to develop their worship according to New Testament practices. But freedom did not solve the problem. People still gazed about as an audience rather than a people centering attention upon God as known in Jesus Christ through the power of the Holy Spirit.

These minister/editors did their best to counteract what they perceived to be happening. Barton W. Stone, upset at seeing that "some were kneeling, some sitting, and others standing," commented that it appeared that some did not kneel for fear of "sullying their fine garments by kneeling." He caustically observed that if the members would keep the floors clean, this would be no problem.[4]

Alexander Campbell insisted that "at the close of all social prayer...the whole congregation that unites in the petitions should, like the primitive Christians say with an audible and clear voice, Amen" (1 Corinthians 14:16, 17). This, Campbell remarked, "is of more importance to the animation and devotion of the social worship than most Christians seem to think."[5]

Another common suggestion for counteracting formalism was to impress upon those partaking of the Lord's Supper to heed the apostle Paul's admonition: "Let a man examine himself and so let him eat of that bread and drink of that cup." Yet, that seemed to turn one's gaze from Christ to self. It is true that in the face of a great monument one may think introspectively, but that comes more as a result of having first absorbed the wonder of it all. Navel gazing is no substitute for gazing around.

All of this appears to be little more than attempting to mend something broken—exasperatedly trying yet something else to hold and center attention in worship.

From today's perspective we find kinship with those gazing Disciples who have gone before us. We may even recognize ourselves in Barton W. Stone's observation that in some churches "as soon as they are dismissed, each flies to his hat—puts it on his head in the household of God, and makes a rush to the door, like children dismissed from the disagreeable toil of learning in a school room."[6]

Building Worship from Identity

Renewal of worship needs to take place in our day as in times of old. Instead of trying to fix our services up at this point and that, the need is to look at worship from a more basic understanding of our heritage. Answers are to be found in recalling how we understand the church and what we mean by worship. Grasping afresh the foundation stones of our identity, we can build worship that truly engages those who gather for Sunday public worship. We can begin to express worship as festive celebration rather than furrowed-brow duty to be performed.

The place to begin thinking about the renewal of worship is the community that assembles about Christ. Christian worship assumes the reality of community. If those who gather about the table do not feel they really belong, they cannot have a sense of owning that worship.

One of my surprises upon entering ministry was to discover that a significant number of church members on the rolls did not really feel they belonged. In conversation they referred to the church as "they" rather than "we." Some of these were nearly charter members of the church, but still lacked a sense of belonging. They remained observers who criticized.

Drawing these detached persons into small, face-to-face groups in which they grew to care for one another had an amazing effect upon their feeling about the larger congregation. Their sense of belonging within the smaller group gave them a feeling of belonging to the whole congregation. All of a sudden worship began to come alive for them. The choir sounded better to them, and, sometimes, even the preaching! They had become owners of worship through a fresh sense of belonging.

The whole service of worship needs to breathe this inclusive spirit that shows love and care. Persons making announcements or sharing joys and concerns are in the process of increasing their sense of ownership. Pastoral prayers that touch deeply the lives of the members not only are heard by God but by those who gratefully say, Amen, in the knowledge the church's minister understands their condition.

The ways worship is expressed must not alienate. I discovered in seeking to use more contemporary language in worship that, although in some ways to get rid of the "thous" and the "ests" was strengthening, other changes were not as helpful. During Lent one year, I printed out a different contemporary version of the Lord's Prayer to pray each Sunday. The congregation was never more grateful for Easter to arrive when they could have their beloved prayer back. I found that although removing some archaisms from worship was an improvement in clarity, their removal evoked a sense of loss upon the part of some.

I had to learn from Aidan Kavanaugh that "the archaic is not the obsolete; it is to the human story what the unconscious is to the human psyche."[7] We hold in the depths of our memory banks treasured ways we learned to worship as children that conveyed the living faith to us. We bring those feelings and associations with us into worship—and rightly so. It is a part of our very identity. We may need to grow from where we were in childhood faith, but in the process we do not need to deny the reality of those early steps of pilgrimage. There is tremendous power in tapping those heartfelt associations that make us know we are at home when we gather on a Sunday.

One problem is that a younger generation does not have the same associations as an older generation. The younger generation may be turned off by what appears to it to be quaint but irrelevant language. A congregation needs to strike a balance, interpreting these different perceptions to one another. There is nothing wrong with a younger generation sharing in the tradition of praying the Lord's Prayer in archaic but majestic words. An older generation can find the reading of the scriptures from the New Revised Standard Version illuminating in a way that adds to, rather than diminishes its worship. In a like manner, when hymn singing is looked at from a community building aspect, it can reflect both contemporary and traditional words and tunes. Unity comes through the feelings evoked.

A striking characteristic of contemporary society is the multiplicity of vocabularies that we speak. Our vocations and subcultures are widely varied, each with its own ways of expression. Going from one cluster to another at a congregation's coffee fellowship following worship is like moving in and out of various tribes, each with its own ways of speech. Sometimes the greatest commonality seems to be the banal subject of the weather.

There is a vocabulary of faith that is rooted in the scriptures. The stories and images of the Bible should become a vital part of the common culture of God's holy community. Throughout worship a conscious effort can be made to develop this common vocabulary of faith and sin; sacrifice and reconciliation; trust, hope, and love. We need to regain the feeling tone of such words as pilgrims and wilderness and principalities and powers. The use of a biblical vocabulary can create a sense of being a part of God's special community that stands distinct from the world. Through the ages, these hallowed words have evoked the depths of feeling that strengthen faith.

Thomas Campbell pointed out the vital relationship of the Bible to congregational worship. He wrote: "This dutiful and religious use of the Bible, (that most precious, sacred record of the wonderful works of God, the only authentic source of all religious information) is inseparably connected with, and indispensably necessary to, the blissful and all-important exercises of prayer and praise. Without this, those exercises must dwindle away to a trite form—must degenerate into lifeless formality. It is from this dutiful and religious use of the divine word, that we derive the proper materials for those holy exercises."[8] Campbell's admonition was in the context of inculcating daily Bible study. It is incumbent upon those who would worship to make the biblical world their context as they enter the church's doors. That has much directly to do with the adequacy of participation in worship.

A Community of Relationships

Worship is owned when there is full participation of those who gather to worship. Disciples proclaim that they practice the priesthood of all believers. They pride themselves upon the fact that lay elders give the consecrating prayers at the Lord's Table. But this idea of an inclusive priesthood goes far beyond this. Priests attend to all aspects of worship.

Early Disciples worship was highly participatory. Alexander Campbell once described a worship service he attended of a congregation of about fifty members where no one was deemed qualified to preach.[9] They choose a senior member to preside. The congregation sings. Someone qualified to read well in public reads a Gospel lesson. A member gives a pastoral prayer. The epistle is read by the one presiding. The president conducts the Lord's Supper with members passing the emblems to one another till all partake. A member is called upon to kneel in public intercessory prayer. The congregation makes an offering. Members respond to the invitation for them to share in mutual edification by reading aloud scripture passages and commenting on them.

The worship closes with various members of the congregation selecting a spiritual song for the congregation to sing. Then the president completes the service by pronouncing an apostolic benediction.

Times have changed and we cannot woodenly copy that model service today. But we can recapture that greater sense of active participation upon the part of those who worship.

We need ever to keep in mind as we work on greater participation of the congregation in worship that the

church is not a community of ideas but of relationships.
When we think of engendering greater participation we
often first look for something that the congregation can say
together. So we develop unison readings and litanies and
call this participation. Although they have their place,
unison readings generally are more a head trip than a
heart trip. Emotion is usually drained from all that is said.
Compare that which is spoken in unison with that which
is sung as a congregation. With singing there is a whole
dimension of feeling added.

Relationships are engendered by symbol, gesture, and
ritual. Caught up in their expression is not only a thought
conveyed but a relation renewed. Disciples are probably
most participatory in their worship not through lay elders
praying, but by the members taking bread and wine and
remembering together why it is they are assembled. Words
spoken in unison are quite insignificant in comparison
with the common signs and symbols and gestures of the
meal itself.

In an effort to be more participatory, many congregations are recovering the ancient tradition of the passing of
the peace. It is a greeting exchanged by some or all of those
present as a sign of fellowship. It goes back in tradition to
New Testament times. The apostle Paul told the Romans,
"Greet one another with a holy kiss" (Romans 16:16).

Our Disciples forebears discussed the pros and cons of
passing the peace in worship. Alexander Campbell opposed it, preferring to extend a right hand of fellowship to
one another. But others took Paul more literally.

Isaac Errett told of an experience that a congregation
in Pittsburgh had in the practice of extending the holy kiss
to all who worshiped. One Sunday morning, as he described it, a "big black" person went forward to take
membership with the church. The Pittsburgh custom was
for the members to march round single file, extend the
right hand of fellowship, and at the same time imprint a resounding "holy kiss" on the convert's cheek.
When the time arrived for the ceremony to begin for the
"brother in black," no one moved. All stood passive.

The situation grew painful. Sensitive people began to wish that holes would open up in the floor through which they might escape. But finally a maiden sister of uncertain age came to the rescue. She rushed to the front, impulsively embraced her colored brother, implanted a fervent kiss on his dusky cheek, and shouted, "I will not deny my brother his privilege."

That expresses something of the power of relationship conveyed in this ancient gesture. It also reveals why, for the wrong reasons, it may be frowned upon. Errett, in telling the story, said that this incident put an end to the holy kiss in the Pittsburgh church.[10]

I suspect that the early practice of the holy kiss developed within the small house churches of the first century where intimacy was already established. It was a quite personal act of either affirmation or reconciliation. In a larger setting where people feel less closely related it loses its original tone.

More commonly today, congregations prefer to extend warm greetings to one another as a gesture of glad caring. Horace T. Allen, Jr., counsels: "In introducing the Peace the people should be given the freedom to be as physical as they wish, remembering that the origin of this rite is reconciliation, not simple affection."[11]

Edifying the Whole Body

Alexander Campbell always made clear that the church's meetings on the Lord's Day were, as he phrased it, "for edification and worship."[12] The word *edify* means to instruct or enlighten so as to encourage moral or spiritual improvement. Campbell and his colleagues resonated to the apostle Paul's admonitions to the Corinthians that all worship should be conducted in such a way "that the church may be edified" (1 Corinthians 14:5, RSV).

Today we think of the word *edify* as meaning to instruct or enlighten so as to encourage moral or spiritual improvement. It meant that for Alexander Campbell, but more. When he said that all of worship must be done for edification, this is how he described it: "The edification and comfort of the brotherhood, their growth in the knowledge of God and of Jesus Christ our Lord, their increase in knowledge of things divine, spiritual, and eternal—in faith, in love, knowledge of things divine, spiritual, and eternal—in faith, in love, in hope, and in spiritual joy, are the points to be kept supremely in view in all the business of the Lord's day in the Lord's house."[13]

Edification included not only enlightenment but the building up of the community "in faith, in love, in hope, and in spiritual joy." Campbell, a translator of scriptures, knew that the root meaning of the Greek word translated edify is to build up. Paul used it to express the way the body of Christ at Corinth needed to be knit together in relationship to God and to one another.

Disciples worship has often emphasized the enlightening aspect of edification to the loss of its relational quality. Worship becomes more participatory when both heart and mind are properly engaged. When today we emphasize the rationality of Disciples as over against a concern for feelings and sentiment, we misread our heritage.

All our Disciples forebears sought to instill a heartfelt trust in God. Alexander Campbell insisted that "the heart" is "the object on which all evangelical arguments are to terminate, and as...the fountain and origin, of all piety and humanity."

"We appreciate nothing in religion," Campbell declared, "which tends not directly and immediately, proximately and remotely, to the purification and perfection of the heart." It is from "a pure heart—love" that "preaching, praying, singing, commemorating, meditation, all issue."[15]

But Alexander Campbell and his colleagues were skeptical of those who sought through exaggerated emotional appeals to transform lives. Campbell believed the results from this approach were ephemeral. Whipped-up emotion, when dissipated, leaves the convert cold, desolate, and forlorn.

Rather, said Campbell, the reformed preachers in their movement "address themselves to the whole man, his understanding, will, and affections, and approach the heart by taking the citadel of the understanding."[16] Walter Scott explained that "the Babel-like confusion" of contending sectarian voices on the frontier required some clear thinking before the heart could adequately be addressed. He concluded, "Reformers must content themselves with getting it into the people's head, that God and his Son loves them."[17]

Preaching for these frontier forebears was a two-part process. First, Campbell said, preachers "address themselves to the understanding, by a declaration or narrative of the wonderful works of God. They state, illustrate, and prove the great facts of the gospel; they lay the whole record before their hearers, [testifying to] what God has done, what he has promised and threatened."[18] This is all appeal to the reasonable understanding of a person.

But, then, second, preachers go on to "exhort their hearers on these premises and persuade them to obey the gospel, to surrender themselves to the guidance and direction of the Son of God."[19] Walter Scott in more lively words explained that: "Exhortations should consist of such things as have a tendency to *move the affections* of those who have believed but not obeyed; they should be elevated, violent, or tender according to the state of the case; bold and lively, striking and animating, containing great and beautiful images, calculated to move the soul and win the world to God."[20]

Alexander Campbell emphasized the edifying nature of preaching by insisting that "the object...of all the preacher's labors is *to impress the moral image of God upon the moral nature of man.*" The preacher's task is "to draw this image upon the heart, to transform the mind of man into the likeness of God in all moral feelings."[21]

A letter written in 1832 by a John C. Ashley describes something of the power of this two-stage preaching. Having just attended a three-day protracted meeting, he wrote he had been thrilled "to see a large congregation melted to tears—not by enthusiastic appeals to passions, but by the impulse of apostolic doctrine."[22]

There is also a fascinating recollection of a frontier preacher who had the awesome responsibility of preaching in the presence of Barton W. Stone. Before the preacher began his sermon, Stone told him, "You know I am deaf—Speak loud—I want to hear every word." The preacher said he "took occasion to speak of the power of faith as well as of that special class of feelings which originates in the heart of him who truly believes." The preacher recalled, "I became somewhat excited in proceeding; and when I had reached a favorite climax, elder Stone advancing with me in every step of the subject and partaking of all my feelings, shouted out aloud, 'Glory be to God!'" The preacher related he had not been prepared for this and it left him confused. "Observing my embarrassment," the preacher said, "he said smilingly, 'Go on, brother, go on!' I resumed the subject and went through."[23]

Just what kind of preaching this may involve can be seen in this description of Walter Scott at work. William Baxter said of Scott that he always "preached Christ" unto his hearers. Of Scott he said: "He always, first appealed to the judgment, and when he thought enough had been said to produce conviction, he used, with great power, the motives of the gospel to induce to action; the promises, to allure; the threatenings, to alarm; and, with a pathos rising from a realizing sense of the danger of his hearers, he would, often with tears, beseech them to accept the offered grace."[24]

These accounts indicate that the mind's approach to emotions generally stopped short of eliciting outward enthusiastic expressions. But preachers walked a fine line of balancing reason and emotion. Both were regarded to be a vital aspect of a Christian's response to the grace of God.

Alexander Campbell's preaching was less emotional. Scott described Campbell's preaching in appreciative but critical terms when he said: "In laying out his work, his statements are simple, clear, and concise; his topics are well and logically arranged, his reasoning calm and deliberate, but full of assurance. His appeals were not very earnest, nor indicative of deep feeling; but, nevertheless, winning and impressive in a high degree."[25]

So, for our forebears, the Lord's Day service was for "edification and worship." Preaching must effect a heartfelt change in the lives of those who hear.

Today there is a paucity of good preaching. Some say we have not great preaching because we no longer have great churches. I dare say the truth lies more nearly in our departure from our Disciples heritage. We have lost the art of preaching the Bible and doctrine in a manner that engages the whole of life—mind and heart.

More truly we have such meager preaching because we have lost our evangelical fervor that touches the depths of life. Our gospel no longer springs from the fountain of baptism and from the fellowship of the table. It is no longer monumental in recalling the simple story of God's great love expressed in the life, death, and resurrection of a living Christ.

Embarrassed by the living Christ grounded in the gospels, proclaimed in the epistles, and witnessed to by the saints of two thousand years, we wander off into therapeutic advice for making it through another week. Seeing the Bible simply as a collection of witnessing accounts of faith, we wonder if their experiences are any more authentic than our own. Seeing the church to which we belong as another support group, we lose the one who upholds with everlasting arms.

Greater participation in worship comes with a greater sense of ownership. The church is truly for belonging. We cannot worship without adequately giving ourselves in heart and mind and soul to one another and to God within this living fellowship. There are important practical steps that can be taken to elicit this participation. But it will come primarily as we recapture a sense that the risen Lord truly does preside at his table and that we are guests who celebrate that presence.

Notes

[1]"Visit to the East," *The Evangelist*, Vol. 10, #4, April 1, 1842, p. 38.
[2]"A Ramble," *The Christian Messenger*, September, 1843, p. 168.
[3]Annie Dillard, *Holy the Firm* (Toronto: Bantam Books, 1979), p. 60.
[4]*The Christian Messenger*, VI (1831), p. 168.
[5]*The Millennial Harbinger*, Extra, Vol. 6, #8 (1835), p. 511.
[6]*The Christian Messenger*, Vol. 6, 1832, p. 132.
[7]Aidan Kavanaugh, *Elements of Rite* (New York: Pueblo Publishing Company, 1982), p. 41.
[8]*The Christian Baptist*, p. 101.
[9]*The Christian System*, p. 351.
[10]J. S. Lamar, *Memoirs of Isaac Errett*, II, p. 240.
[11]"The Grace of Gesture," *Reformed Liturgy and Music*, Winter 1987, p. 32.
[12]*The Christian Baptist*, p. 175.
[13]*The Millennial Harbinger*, Extra, Vol. 6, #8 (1835), p. 507.
[14]*The Christian System*, p. 75.
[15]*Ibid.*, p. 263.
[16]*Ibid.*, p. 77.
[17]*The Evangelist*, Vol. 6 (1838), p. 183.
[18]*The Christian System*, p. 314.
[19]*Ibid.*
[20]*The Evangelist*, Vol. 1 (1831), p. 139.
[21]*The Christian System*, p. 319.
[22]*The Evangelist*, Vol. 1 (1832) p. 263.
[23]Rogers, *The Biography of Elder Barton Warren Stone*, p. 304.
[24]Baxter, *Life of Elder Walter Scott*, p. 326f.
[25]*Ibid.*, p. 347.

8

Characterizing
Disciples Worship

Thinking about the way Disciples worship, what best describes it? Sometimes attempts are made to fit Disciples into one of a variety of church family categories. These include such traditions as Eastern Orthodox, Roman Catholic, reformed, evangelical, Anglican, free church, or mystical. Where do Disciples fit?

Some Disciples have seen themselves as an expression of a free church, but upon closer examination, scholars do not agree on what a free church is. Others have recognized something of reformed, catholic, and evangelical strains in the way Disciples worship.

Although such discussions may have some academic value in placing Disciples worship in its broader ecumenical context, they are not likely to help congregations to characterize their worship.

Disciples worship cannot be easily boxed, wrapped, and neatly labeled. To do so is likely to distort the truth about it. A problem with categories is that as soon as the label is applied, the tendency is then to proceed to make misleading deductions from it. Someone says, "Since Disciples worship is in the free-church tradition, then this and that and the other thing ought also to be true about its worship." They quickly depart from the realities of congregational life and become prescriptive according to category.

More helpful is to review Disciples heritage of worship and describe its broad characteristics. This will give a more vital sense of who Disciples are. We can leave it to others to figure out what to make of it in the larger schema of church history.

As Disciples worship defies neat categories, it also resists description in logical sequence. Some things need to be said all at the same time. Since that cannot be done, we shall name the characteristics as they come to mind, trusting their interrelations will become apparent as they unfold.

1. *The Disciples congregation owns its worship.* When Disciples think of themselves as being an expression of a free church, they generally mean that no church body beyond the local congregation has the authority to prescribe its worship.

Alexander Campbell put it differently. He emphasized the competence of a congregation to study the scriptures, determine how it should worship, and then conduct it under the authority of the living Christ. Worship is free because it is under the disciplined constraint of scripture, and of the one in whose name the worshipers meet.

Alexander Campbell, through careful study of the apostolic writings of the New Testament, identified "certain ordinances delivered to the church by her exalted Redeemer, which she is constantly to observe in all her meetings to worship him." These invariable ordinances for

Lord's Day worship are: "that songs of praise, that prayers, supplications, and thanksgivings are to be preserved before the throne of grace, in the name of our Great High Priest; that the Scriptures are to be read—that the word is to be inculcated, and exhortations tendered—that he Lord's death is to be commemorated—that the poor saints are to be remembered—and that discipline, when necessary, is to be attended to."

Beyond these essentials, other matters of worship are "left to the discretion of the brotherhood, and to that expediency...for which no unchangeable ritual or formulary could possibly have been instituted."[1] These are matters that D. R. Dungan, in a later time referred to as having "been left largely to the consecrated common sense."[2]

Something of the way a congregation comes to own its worship is illustrated in a letter of inquiry to Walter Scott by Bro. Strong of Kentucky in 1833: "Ought a church to meet, and keep the ordinances, though it has no elders and deacons?" Scott replied affirmatively, concluding, "Go on, beloved; be strong, hold forth the Word of Truth, to all around, and the very God of peace be with you...."[3]

The Disciples congregation owns its worship. It exercises its competency to know the ordinances of Christ and to fulfill them. It does so under the authority of the living Christ who dwells in its midst. It expresses its ownership through the full participation of all its members throughout the service.

2. *Disciples worship is trinitarian.* Both Thomas Campbell and his son, Alexander, defined worship in trinitarian terms. As we have noted, Thomas Campbell quite early declared, "we worship the Father, through the son, by the Spirit." Campbell's son, Alexander, later reaffirmed this understanding of worship by declaring: "All worship, whether prayer or praise, ultimately terminates upon, or is addressed to, the Father of angels and of men. God is worshipped *through* the Messiah as an intercessor, and *by* the Spirit of God in our hearts prompting and maturing the acceptable desires."[4]

Some Disciples may think their heritage opposes the trinity. Alexander Campbell, favoring Bible names for Bible things, preferred not to use that word. He further believed that its formulations had become so filled with extra-biblical meaning that they had become divisive. But hear him on this subject: "My principal objection to the popular doctrine of 'the Trinity' is not that it is either irrational, or unscriptural, to infer that there are three Divine persons in one Divine nature. That these three equally have one thought, purpose, will, and operation, and so one God....I object not to this doctrine because it is contrary to reason, or revelation, but because of the metaphysical technicalities, the unintelligible jargon, the unmeaning language of the orthodox creed on this subject, and the interminable war of words without ideas to which this word Trinity has given birth."[5]

More positively, Campbell insisted: "A religion not honoring God the Father of all—not relying upon the person, mission and death of the Word incarnate—not inspired, cherished, animated and inflamed by the Holy Spirit dwelling in my soul, is a cheat, a base counterfeit, and not that athletic, strong and invincible thing which armed the martyr's soul against all the terrors that earth and hell could throw around the Redeemer, his cause and people."[6]

And, of course, baptism, using the scripturally ordained trinitarian formula, was an ordinance to be obeyed.

The whole structure of worship is based upon the worship of God through Christ in the Spirit. The congregation centers upon the worship of God through the revelation of Jesus Christ made a living reality by the Spirit.

This trinitarian understanding reaching back into New Testament times keeps Disciples worship in focus. Although worship is centered in Jesus Christ about the Lord's Table, it is not a Jesusolatry. It is through Jesus Christ that a congregation approaches God and receives God's abounding grace. Apart from the Holy Spirit, worship would be a dead memorial of things past. The Spirit enlivens the worshiper to God's present reality.

This trinitarian understanding of God serves always to balance congregational worship. Much worship flounders on the distortion of this relationship. Quite generally, Disciples worship acknowledges this triune understanding of God in its hymns, prayers, and sacraments. In singing the "Gloria Patri," Disciples go beyond the ancient worship of the Father through the Son by the Holy Spirit; they ascribe glory to all three persons equally. Occasionally Disciples pray to Christ and often direct their praise to him. In so doing, they exhibit fresh reasons for understanding the intentions of creedal statements.

3. *The context of Disciples worship is the story of a gracious God.* Disciples affirm with the apostle Paul that human beings are saved by grace through faith. Faith is directed toward a person—Jesus the Christ whose story of life, death, and resurrection is told in the New Testament.

Worship at its heart proclaims the good news of God's favor. Each of its monumental ordinances—Lord's Day, Lord's Supper, and baptism—heralds the same good news. Each calls attention to the mighty acts of God in Jesus Christ to redeem the world. Worshipers by sharing in these monumental acts become alive to that redemption effected long ago. Through the power of the Holy Spirit, worshipers receive that once-and-for-all grace for themselves.

Baptism is, Thomas Campbell maintained, "the first instituted act of Christian worship." It is "an expression of faith and obedience on the part of the baptized."[7] It is the first "therefore" of faith. Baptism is not a good work one does to effect one's salvation, but a means of receiving God's grace. Alexander Campbell remarked that "in baptism we are passive in every thing but in giving our consent."[8] Baptism is a rejoicing in God's gracious love.

4. *In Disciples worship, ordinances are the means for enjoying communion with God.* When Disciples forebears left their Presbyterian churches to reform the church, they brought with them much of their heritage. Their

Westminster Confession asked the question: "What is the
chief end of Man?" The specified answer was: "To glorify
God and enjoy him forever." This was how the Campbells
understood salvation. Alexander Campbell stated: "In the
present administration of the Kingdom of God, *faith is the
PRINCIPLE, and ordinances the MEANS, of all spiritual
enjoyment.*" He said this was so "because all the wisdom,
power, love, mercy, compassion, or *grace of God* is in the
ordinances of the Kingdom of Heaven; and if all grace be
in them it can only be enjoyed through them."[9] He then
gave an astounding list of ways God bestows God's favor
through acts of worship.

Worship is objective, centering trustful faith in God as
revealed in Jesus Christ. It is subjective in the sense that
the one who is worshiped showers gifts of grace upon the
worshipers as reflexive action. Worship is not a quid-pro-
quo arrangement in which the worshiper manipulates
God so as to receive favors. Rather, worship is communion
with God in which God gives God's self to those who will
share in God's life. That communion is the enjoyment of
God. Ultimately, the issue of objective and subjective
worship melts away into the blessings of divine-human
fellowship.

Thus, the whole of congregational worship, in each of
its parts and together, is sacramental in nature—a means
of God's grace. The orientation of Sunday worship is that
of entrusting ourselves to God and enjoying every moment
of it.

5. *The Lord's Supper is the constituting factor in Disciples worship, shaping all of its life.* Studying the practice
of worship in New Testament times, Disciples mothers
and fathers in the faith concluded that Christians gathered on the first day of the week to share together in the
Lord's Supper. The evidence probably is not as clear as
they thought in this regard. However, there is scholarly
consensus today that this was likely the case. Alexander
Campbell, speaking on behalf of his movement, declared:
"The breaking of the one loaf, and the joint participation of

the cup of the Lord, in commemoration of the Lord's death, usually called 'the Lord's Supper,' is an instituted part of the worship and edification of all Christian congregations in all their stated meetings."[10]

Although there is a multiplicity of means of receiving God's grace in worship, they all lead to the real presence of Christ in its midst. Christ is present in a special way not otherwise known to his people. Indeed, it is Christ through communion at this table who constitutes this assembly of people as his church.

The whole service of worship is shaped and given meaning by this central Lord's Table action. From the call to worship through the benediction, every part reverberates to the partaking of Christ's holy meal. The demeanor of joy and gladness radiates from the realization that here in this place is a festal board spread by the Lord of hosts.

6. *Normative Sunday congregational worship includes the preaching of the Word and sharing in the Lord's Supper.* Some Disciples misunderstand their forebears' emphasis upon the Lord's Supper as depreciating the necessity of preaching. This is far from the case. Participation in the Lord's Supper normatively presupposes the preaching of the Word. Preaching is one of the essential ordinances of worship.

It is true that, confronted by frontier conditions, some early congregations did not always have preaching. There was a paucity of trained leadership. When no one capable of preaching was present, members of the congregation read scripture together and shared with one another their insights. That was the best they could do. But they always preferred to have worthy preaching as a part of their Lord's Day worship.

The purpose of preaching was of one part with the object of the Lord's Supper. Alexander Campbell counseled preachers to keep in mind that the all-important consideration in preaching is "to impress the moral image of God upon the moral nature of man." Their purpose was to "draw this image upon the heart, to transform the mind of man into the likeness of God in all moral feelings." By proclaiming the gospel story and interpreting it in the light of apostolic doctrine, Campbell concluded, "there is written upon the understanding, and engraved upon the heart, the will, or law, or character, of our Father who is in heaven."[11]

Preaching, apart from the Lord's Supper, tends to be less experiential of the presence of God in Christ. The Lord's Supper, apart from preaching, tends greatly to limit the rich meaning of the symbolism enacted. There is the need for both word and sign. The preaching of the word preceding the partaking of the Lord's Supper reminds worshipers afresh of the profound meaning and relevance of what they do at that meal.

7. *Disciples worship looks to the fulfillment of God's future.* Early Disciples worship was conducted with great anticipation for the ultimate fulfillment of all of life. The week-by-week imprinting of the image of God upon the hearts and wills of the worshipers each Sunday looked to their full regeneration yet completely to be realized.

The Lord's Supper is food for a journey not yet completed. So Alexander Campbell said of it: "It is a religious feast; a feast of joy and gladness; the happiest occasion, and the sweetest antepast on earth of the society and entertainment of heaven, that mortals meet with on their way to the true Canaan."[12] That image of "the true Canaan" had a double meaning for these worshipers. They looked to "the true Canaan," which is the promised land of God's fulfillment of God's kingdom here on earth. They looked to a meaningful fulfillment of history in which God's will is done on earth as it is in heaven.

At the same time, they pilgrimaged toward "the new Canaan" of a heavenly existence of eternal communion with God in Christ. Campbell observed the effect the Lord's Supper has upon the believer: "It cherishes the peace of God, and inscribes the image of God upon his heart, and leaves not out of view the revival of his body from the dust of death, and its glorious transformation to the likeness of the Son of God."[13]

Without this lively anticipation of God's future, worship becomes static and void of purpose. Worship is hopeful. To my mind, the climactic statement of a Sunday service of worship comes immediately following the recalling of Jesus' words instituting the Lord's Supper. We add, with the apostle Paul, "For as often as you eat this bread and drink the cup, you proclaim the Lord's death until he comes" (1 Corinthians 11:26). That keeps the tension between who we are and what we are to become.

8. *Disciples worship addresses the whole person—understanding, will, and emotions.* Alexander Campbell, accused of belittling experiential religion, once retorted: "A religion that fills not the conscience with peace, the heart with love, the affections with joy, the soul with hope, and the life with good works, is not worth an untimely fig."[14] Worship affects the whole person and all of living.

Campbell insisted that the heart is "the object on which all evangelical arguments are to terminate, and as the *fons et principium*, the fountain and origin, of all piety and humanity."[15] Reason, of course, has its place. Walter Scott explained that people's hearts had been so distorted by endless religious wrangling that these frontier reformers "must content themselves with getting it into the people's head, that God and his Son loves them."[16]

Disciples worship recognizes that worship is embodied in real human beings whose flesh includes reason, feelings, and will. Christian formation takes place through what we experience—matters going far beyond the powers of understanding. Yet, without adequate reflection upon those experiences, Christians tend to get lost in the recesses of their still wayward hearts. On the other hand, worship centered upon reason, separated from experience, tends to lead toward sterile if not demonic rationalizations. Worship is a matter of the head and the heart. Of this Disciples forebears were certain.

9. *Disciples worship is done decently and in order.* When in the spring of 1835 Walter Scott visited the church

that had been founded by Barton W. Stone at Georgetown, Kentucky, he had this observation to make about its Lord's Day worship: "Never did I see the business of the day go off with greater decency, or greater order."[17]

The manner in which worship takes place is important. Everything must be done in the light of the apostolic admonition, "Let all things be done decently and in order" (1 Corinthians 14:40, KJV).

What Walter Scott liked about the Georgetown service is what would have pleased any of this movement's leaders. The prayers, said Scott, "were Christian, and so much the more because they were short." He particularly praised the reading of the scriptures by a Dr. Hatch "who," he said, "may be pronounced one of the very best readers of English." Scott liked the way the prayers of blessing of bread and cup were done, saying: "The persons officiating did not seem to think that they had arisen to pray at the sects, or for every thing and person within the wide compass of the world. It was thanks for the bread, it was thanks for the wine, and for Him who is the bread and the wine."

The concern here was not for genteel manners. These leaders were, rather, concerned for genuineness of piety. Going through the actions of Christ's ordinances without clarity of understanding and genuine feeling was a formalism void of all substance. True worship issues from a heart that grasps the tremendous significance of trusting God and receiving afresh God's grace.

For Campbell the whole feeling tone and demeanor of true worshipers was appropriately determined by reference to the fact that Christ is truly present in the midst of the assembly. Campbell pointed out that the congregation "in all its movements ought never to lose sight of that dignity and decorum which accord with its high and holy relations to its exalted head"—Jesus Christ.[18]

Marks of decency and order in Disciples tradition are intelligibility, simplicity, and beauty. What is said and done must make sense. It must be spoken clearly and with thought. It sees worship as a gift to be simple. Jesus decried those who camouflaged a barren soul with much speech. Jesus' words were simple and direct. All is infused with beauty appropriate to a festive occasion. Walter Scott particularly lifted up the beauty of song in worship.

"Let all be done in decency and in order." That meant for early Disciples acting out one's heartfelt faith appropriately in the presence of the living Christ. When this happens, believers truly worship.

10. *Disciples worship is grounded in New Testament scripture as the source for faith and practice.* Alexander Campbell emphasizing this point stated: "For to the end of time, we shall have no other revelation of the Spirit, no other New Testament, no other Savior, and no other religion than we now have, when we understand, believe and practice the doctrine of Christ delivered to us by his apostles."[19]

Decisions as to all aspects of life in the church were made by these ministerial leaders in the light of their understanding of New Testament Christianity. Some central aspects of worship were identified as essential. Many matters were left open to what expediency requires with changing circumstances. These early leaders were wrong in assuming that Jesus had given careful instructions to the apostles as to how to conduct worship. New Testament evidence does not support that contention. But they stood within the whole of Christian tradition in recognizing the New Testament as the reference point for all discussions of proper faith and practice.

This remains true today. Disciples may reject the wooden interpretations of the past, but they treasure the New Testament as the source book and standard of worship. Theirs is an apostolic faith. The Hebrew scriptures are important to them as they were to the apostles. But Disciples view them through the eyes of apostolic faith in Jesus who is the Christ.

Notes

[1]*The Millennial Harbinger*, Extra, Vol. 6, #8 (1835), p. 509.

[2]D. R. Dungan, "The Lord's Supper," *The Old Faith Restated*, n.d., p. 231.

[3]*The Evangelist*, Vol. 2 (1833), p. 62.

[4]"Christian Psalmody—No. V," *The Millennial Harbinger*, Vol. 15 (1844), p. 407.

[5]*The Millennial Harbinger*, 1833, p. 155.

[6]Quoted by Robert Richardson, *Memoirs of Alexander Campbell*, II, p. 483.

[7]*The Christian Baptist*, p. 99. The initials T. W., identifying the article's author, were a pseudonym for Thomas Campbell.

[8]*The Millennial Harbinger*, Series III, IV (1847), 5, p. 250.

[9]*The Christian System*, p. 185f.

[10]*Ibid.*, p. 332.

[11]*Ibid.*, p. 319.

[12]*Ibid.*, p. 175.

[13]*The Christian Baptist*, p. 175.

[14]*The Millennial Harbinger*, Vol. I (1830), p. 260.

[15]*The Christian System*, p. 262.

[16]"Evangelist of the True Gospel," *The Evangelist*, Vol. 6, 1838, p. 183.

[17]*The Evangelist*, Vol 4 (1835) p. 111.

[18]*The Millennial Harbinger*, Extra, Vol 6., Number 8, 1835, p. 508.

[19]*The Christian Baptist*, p. 128.